Dedicated to all the hard-working independent cleaning business owners who remember when the trusted local contractor reigned supreme.....and want to discover how they can again!

DISCOVER THE
GURU *in* YOU®

Clean Guru reveals how two desperate, flat-broke friends from high school quickly built a highly profitable $2,000,000/yr. cleaning business in...

DISCOVER THE GURU in YOU ®

The **7 INSIDER SECRETS** to **FINDING, LANDING** And **KEEPING** Profitable Cleaning Jobs!

Plus 89 of our very best marketing, selling and profit tips ever!

"Discover The Guru In YOU!" 24 Hr. Challenge!!

If YOU can absorb the incredible amount of insider information jam-packed into this book in one day, that's right, just 24 HOURS - "scream" to us by e-mail "I DISCOVERED THE GURU!", and get 24 DAYS of the CleanBid Program...ABSOLUTELY FREE! *

* offer good for first-time users only, *so if that's you*, ACT NOW!

Table of Contents:

PART II - HOW TO LAND

Insider Secret #4: Aim To Be NEXT 101

PART III – HOW TO KEEP

Introduction:

WARNING: Things have changed.

You know it. We know it. And every cleaning business out there today can see and feel it.

What is it? It's this…

The <u>old</u> ways of growing a successful cleaning business just DON'T work any more.

20 years ago, when we started our business, nearly anyone could have a pretty sizable customer list just by knocking on doors, and then cleaning the buildings well.

Really, it was about that simple.

Hard work and a good reputation would get you more jobs, and at prices that made you a tidy profit!

Not any more.

Today, there are <u>three</u> changes killing the once-strong, independent cleaning businesses across the country, which used to be the backbone of this industry.

1. The first's the economy.

No question about it; companies desperate to cut costs, not only don't spare office-cleaning when it comes time to cut, but, often make it the first thing on the chopping block.

2. The second's the widespread use of illegal workers by unscrupulous cleaning contractors.

Here, everyone suffers.

From the *sometimes* unsuspecting building owners, exposed to potential legal problems to the frustrated, legitimate cleaning contractors, who are justifiably angry having to deal with the ridiculously low prices offered by these unscrupulous contractors.

3. The third change destroying independent cleaning businesses is the rise of *empty-promising* national management companies and *slick-marketing* cleaning franchises, whose business strategy seems no more complicated than this:

Low-ball the price to get the job... then quickly dump it on some desperate, local guy who needs the work!

(And, oh yeah, good luck to that guy on having enough hours to clean the place, or trying to make a profit!)

Sadly, it's about that simple.

But who's kidding who? Those national maintenance management companies know in this economy, they'll get plenty of struggling building owners and managers to "bite" fast n' hard on their price-slashing pitch!

And, those cleaning franchises know it too - as they push their glossy brochures and bottom-basement prices!

But here's the catch:

Frantic, knee-jerk decisions to drastically cut costs without getting the facts first (verifying references, as well as confirming quality, training and management methods) quickly backfire when *frustrated* customers discover they've been sold a bag of empty promises!

Well, WE'VE HAD ENOUGH OF IT!

And <u>this</u> book is one way we're <u>striking</u> back!

But, to understand why we feel this strongly, we need to take you back in time....

You see, we started out with next to nothing, like a lot of folks out there today. In fact, *less than nothing* - frequently having to use <u>credit</u> <u>cards</u> to cover payrolls and monthly bills!

But, we got "lucky".

We discovered and implemented a set of *insider* strategies - quickly moving us out of the **red** of debt and into the **black** of profitability!

Here's the good news:

Those same "game-changing" strategies, the ones we used to build a profitable $2,000,000.00 cleaning business, are described in <u>detail</u> in this book.

But, back to the story...

Unfortunately, while we were doing well, *many others were not.*

That's right, the <u>shocking</u> number of *heartbreaking stories* told by hard-working cleaning contractors, describing how they'd lost many of their oldest and most loyal accounts to one of those *slick-marketing*, low-balling "big guys"....grew louder and LOUDER.

Finally, it became impossible for us to stand quietly by.

We decided to "level the playing field"... so <u>independent cleaning contractors</u> could compete and win against these "big guys".

It became our #1 MISSION!!

So, in late 2008, finding we simply could not run our own company and help other independent contractors to the degree we wanted… we made the difficult decision to sell our own cleaning business.

Fortunately, once we had made the decision, we had no difficulty in doing so, and soon sold it for a solid gain… providing us lasting financial security.

And, sure, we're proud. But, we don't tell you this to brag. No, we say it for one reason and one reason only; because we know…

…<u>YOU can do it too</u>, but only if you grow your business <u>the</u> <u>right</u> <u>way</u>.

We believe the set of strategies revealed in **"Discover The Guru In YOU!"** ™ – The 7 Insider Secrets To Finding, Landing and Keeping MORE Profitable Cleaning Jobs NOW … <u>is</u> <u>that</u> <u>right</u> <u>way</u>!

Interested? Great! *But before we begin…*

We're <u>NOT</u> For EVERYBODY!!

That's right; before we start, we should make it clear… we're definitely NOT for everybody.

If you'd <u>rather</u> do things the **hard way**… because some so-called "expert" said you had to spend more than a few painful years, like they did, desperately begging to learn the "ins and outs" of the cleaning biz… <u>and</u> <u>you</u> <u>believed</u> <u>them</u>!?... we're probably NOT for you!

Or *if you're <u>satisfied</u>* with how **fast** you're growing, and are **happy** with the money you're making now, then, we're definitely NOT what you're looking for.

And, finally, *if you're <u>not</u> open to change*, or are easily offended by new ideas, explained in a direct, **pull-no-punches** approach, then we're probably not going to be your cup-of-tea either!

Feel free to look elsewhere...*no hard feelings.*

But, if you <u>do</u> want to "get your hands" on the strategies that really work, and if you're ready to start NOW to create a FAST growing and PROFITABLE cleaning business... then, my friend, you're <u>definitely</u> in the right place!

What you'll read in this book may surprise, or even *<u>shock</u>* you, but it may be just what you need to hear...or more importantly, need to know!

That's it then.

We're going to "yank", not gently pull back, the curtains to reveal the *behind-the-scenes*, insider secrets to success in the cleaning business.

At our company, Clean Guru LLC, we believe if you take <u>these strategies</u> and combine them with your own drive and determination, you can, as the name of the book suggests, Discover the Guru in YOU!

That's right, we'll reveal how we did it, and more importantly, how YOU can do it too! Still interested? OK, let's get started...

What's the SECRET?

Well, that's really <u>the</u> question, isn't it, "What's the secret?"

So, let's just get it out of the way now. Here it is then, listen carefully... drum roll please....

The secret is... **<u>there isn't one.</u>**

We wish there were.

Really, life would be so much easier. We could simply whisper it in your ear and *poof*, like magic, you'd be effortlessly landing new accounts, filling new jobs and sitting back watching the profits roll in...all from a single lap-top computer.

But, we can't.

You see, there simply isn't ONE, all-powerful secret. But don't be discouraged.

In fact, be glad!

You see, if there was only <u>one</u> secret to this business, you might be able to build a wildly successful business at first, but <u>you wouldn't be able to keep it</u>...at least not for long.

Let us tell you a story...

Years ago, we went to an industry convention for cleaning companies. At lunch, a fellow cleaning business owner attending the event for the first time asked us, "How much business do you guys *do* a year?"

We told him; but it's what he asked <u>next</u> we'll never forget.

He leaned in close, and armed with a tiny index card, readied a ballpoint pen, and said... *"So, how did you do that?"*

"Do what?" we replied.

"Get that big...how'd you do that?" he responded

Now, don't misunderstand - we liked this guy. He was interested, open and ready to learn. And we tried to tell him a few of the most important things he might want to try when he got back home.

But there certainly wasn't just ONE thing, ONE secret, we could pass along to him to transform his cleaning business. (In fact, there wasn't enough room on <u>both</u> sides of his index card to do that!)

But he had the right idea:

- Be open.

- Ask someone who has already done what you want to do.

We hope the things we told him that day helped him reach his goals.

But, again, here's the thing....

It's actually <u>good</u> that it takes <u>not</u> one, but a number of powerful strategies to grow a successful cleaning business.

Why?

Because, if it only took one trick to be successful - anyone and everyone could do it, *almost immediately*, and you'd have to fight off the wave of threatening competitors with a stick.

But, you don't have to. *Here's why*:

In the pages to follow, we reveal <u>not one</u>, but SEVEN powerful strategies designed to quickly and easily **separate you** from your competitors, **position you** at the head of the pack, and then, **keep you** ahead of them.

PICTURE Something!

Stop for a second, and get a clear picture in your mind of how you'd like life to be...in your cleaning business

Seriously.

Take just a moment to <u>really</u> think about it. If you could make a wish and see it *magically come true*, what would you wish your cleaning business looked like?

Done?

Ok, now, was any of <u>this</u> in your picture?

1. Having LOTS of customers.

2. Having those customers LOVE your company and cleaners.

3. Having those cleaners not only know <u>what</u> to do, but really <u>want</u> to do a great job for those customers.

4. Having FUN each day.

5. Having TIME to just "kick back" and relax both after work and on weekends! And we mean <u>really</u> relax - <u>not</u> having to always worry half-to-death whether or not you're even going to make it!

*Oh, and wait, there's <u>one more</u>... and, **YES, we'll say it**,*

6. Getting paid an amount that does a <u>whole</u> lot MORE… than just cover your bills!

You heard right.

Your cleaning business is <u>supposed</u> to cover all your expenses, <u>plus</u> give you enough profit for financial security and relaxing vacations NOW, and then someday, a wonderful retirement!

It's <u>not</u> too much to ask for. It's the way it <u>should</u> be.

So, were any of those things in your picture too? We hope so; because that's the kind of fun and profitable cleaning business you can have!

Is any other kind really worth having?

But, to have that kind of cleaning business, the fast growing, fun and profitable kind, you need to start by asking some questions; the <u>right</u> questions. And the first one is this:

Who do you want to clean...and <u>why</u>?

That's right, deciding who you want to clean is one of the big secrets to having a cleaning business like the one you pictured. Put another way, what <u>kind</u> of accounts (jobs) can be counted on to give you plenty of the following:

<u>Time, Income and Freedom</u>

Well, to have a business that gives you <u>those</u> things, you'll need cleaning accounts (jobs) that:

1. Give you **steady income** - *rather than feast or famine*

2. Are **easy to staff** - *rather than constant turnover*

3. Are **easy to manage** - *rather than ongoing employee "headaches"*

4. Give you a shot at <u>extra</u> "specialty" type work now and then - *the kind that can be a highly profitable addition to your regular monthly check!*

Hint: Compare these different types of jobs: Construction Cleaning? Retail Floor Strip/Wax Jobs? Apt/Condo Move In/Out? Office-Cleaning? Restaurant Cleaning? Residential?

PART I
HOW TO FIND

INSIDER SECRET #1
Know WHO You WANT to Clean and WHY!

1. WHO You WANT to Clean

OK, let's get right to it, because the sooner we answer <u>this</u> question, the sooner you can have the kind of cleaning business you've always dreamed of.

Think of it this way…

What kind of accounts would… give you a steady income, be easy to staff, easy to manage and give you a "shot" at extra work year round?

Or, put yet another way,

What <u>kind</u> of accounts would let you quickly grow a large, profitable and stable cleaning business?

Well, here was the answer for us… **office cleaning!**

That's right, office-cleaning. And to be clear; by that we mean, the standard, routine cleaning (i.e. vacuuming, dusting, trash removal) of offices, hallways, conference rooms, break rooms and restrooms etc.

Specifically; 3-5 nights per week, office-cleaning, performed in the early evening, for owner-occupied professional, medical, industrial and manufacturing buildings over 7,500 square feet and within a 50-mile radius of our office.

You may want to take a second to re-read that because <u>every</u> part of it was, and is, important.

It became our target market - *our niche!*

So, a typical example of a building in our target market might be a manufacturing company in a local industrial park, where we would clean the front office area, as well as the plant offices, restrooms, lockers and lunchroom Monday - Friday from 6:00 PM - 9:30 PM.

First, we want to be perfectly clear...

Our answer doesn't have to be your answer. There's <u>more</u> than one road to get to a destination.

Your answer - your target market or niche, may be floor maintenance for grocery stores and retail centers, construction cleaning for general contractors, residential maid services for homes, or make-ready or move in/out jobs for apartment managers.

And, if you can grow <u>as fast as you'd like</u> in those target markets, <u>as profitably as you'd like</u>, with your customer base being <u>as stable as you'd like</u>, thereby giving you the **time, income** and **freedom** you want, then... <u>great</u>; *more power to you!*

But, for us, office-cleaning was *"the ticket"*.

Nothing is perfect. But, *in general*, routine office-cleaning was the right target market for us for several reasons:

- It gave us a steady, recurring monthly income.

- It allowed us to grow! grow! grow!

- It was relatively easy to staff.

- It was relatively easy to manage.

- It gave us extra specialty work year round.

By the way, if the description of our target market sounds very specific, it is! We find the more specific our goals are, the better chance we have of achieving them.

And, really, isn't that true for everyone?

So, we determined to aggressively go after our target market, while respectfully <u>passing</u> on, whenever possible, "other" types of cleaning.

The impact of this decision was huge!

It sharply focused our company and helped us quickly create a stable, profitable business, like the one we pictured.

You can use this same strategy to FOCUS your company.

2. Who You DON'T

Now, let's talk about deciding who you <u>don't</u> want to clean ...and why.

It's interesting; when we first started out, we would take on nearly <u>any</u> kind of cleaning job, and some things that weren't really cleaning at all.

Let's see, we:

- *stripped* and refinished floors in groceries, hardware stores and beauty salons

- *resealed* concrete in the plant area of a commercial laundry

- *opened* up a reception hall for weddings; and, oh yeah... *hooked up the beer taps and pop canisters too,*

- *mowed* the lawn and took the trash to the curb at a local union hall

So, as you can see, we were running around doing a virtual "hodge-podge" of things.

Frankly, it wasn't going so well.

We just couldn't seem to grow. In looking back, we now realize it was because we had our hands "full" just trying to keep up with the crazy schedules and unusual demands of our various kinds of customers. It was simply too much.

Like "hamsters on a wheel", we were running as fast as we could, but not really getting anywhere. We decided something had to change if we ever hoped to grow.

So we made a list of the kinds of cleaning we didn't want:

1. Nothing less than twice per week.

2. No one-time only jobs.

3. No jobs where all we do is the floors.

4. Nothing where we can't get a key to get in and out.

5. Nothing where we can't start cleaning until very late at night.

6. No odd-ball jobs not relating to cleaning. No more!

Those were some of the ones on our list. Your list may be completely different, but you should at least have one.

It is not laziness, or an unwillingness to help a potential customer.

It's survival!

You simply cannot be everything to everyone. And, frankly, the sooner you decide what the rules are for doing business with you, the better.

That might sound harsh. *This idea is difficult to accept for many of us.*

We're taught from when we're very young to help anyone; anyway we can, anytime we can. So it's hard for us to get our "head around" this idea of limiting what we'll do for our customers.

But, here's the thing:

You have to do it… if you ever want things to run smoothly.

You shouldn't have to run around frantically, having to change everything about your company, just so you never have to turn down a prospect's request; no matter what it is they want.

You deserve better and frankly... *so do your customers!*

Just because someone says they need "cleaning" doesn't automatically mean they're the right customer for you, or for that matter, that you're the right contractor for them.

Focus on a **specific** type of customer and you can become a *specialist* at providing a **specific** kind of cleaning for a **specific** kind of customer or building. (Incidentally, a specialist can charge more… *just ask your local heart surgeon!*)

And then, you might also have a chance to actually delight your customers and "have a life" outside of your cleaning business. Plus, it will let you focus your marketing efforts at one, or at most, a few types of niches. However, you may feel like asking…

"But, won't I miss out on a lot of jobs that way?"

Yes, by deciding what you won't do, you will be turning down some work. It's the price you pay to get focused on the kind of jobs you really want to do.

By the way, don't misunderstand. It may take you a while to make this changeover - a changeover to servicing only your primary target market.

And you may want to hold on to all of your current accounts, no matter what kind they are, forever, or at least until you're able to replace them with enough profitable ones from your new target market.

Plus, to be fair, **we made exceptions.**

For example, for years we continued to provide early morning day porter services, clean plants, and even pick weeds <u>for some of our clients</u>.

BUT, *here's the thing*, and this is <u>important</u>:

It's <u>one</u> thing to agree to pick a few weeds out front once a month for a $3,500/ mo. smooth running medical building, *and quite another*, to have to arrange for mowing the lawn at a small office you clean once a week for $165/mo.

AND, it's <u>one</u> thing to clean artificial plants occasionally for a large 5x/ week facility for $4,700/mo., *and quite another*, to have to figure out how to get a trained floor crew to show up late at night at a hair salon, to buff the floors once a week for $150.

You get the idea.

3. Property Managed OR Owner Occupied?

Which do we prefer?

Short answer? Owner Occupied.

There, you have it; done, class dismissed. But, all kidding aside, we could learn a few things by looking at this question.

First, let's re-state it this way:
Which is better to go after, if you want to grow quickly and profitably
- ....*property managed or owner occupied buildings?*
To answer <u>that</u> question, let's tackle each one separately.

On one hand, there's property-managed buildings where, of course, a property manager is responsible for "managing" the building for the "owners".

In this arrangement, the property manager's goal is to basically keep the building as close to fully occupied as possible and running as smoothly as possible, and to be <u>blunt</u>, *for as little as possible!*

Now, *hold your horses*, we know many of you can quickly give us examples of how this <u>isn't</u> true - where a wise property manager actually hired a janitorial cleaning service that came in quite a bit higher than the rest of the bidders.

Fine, it happens - *once in a while.*

We're not here to argue the point. But, in our experience, it just doesn't happen very often, at least <u>not</u> often enough to our way of thinking, to justify spending much marketing time or money on them.

Again, are there exceptions to this "rule"? Sure.

In fact, we cleaned buildings for property managers for years. But the big difference for us was, in those cases, we landed them on <u>our</u> <u>terms</u>.

What terms are those?

First, we had to be able to provide a level of cleaning we were proud to attach our name to. Notice, we didn't say "perfect" cleaning, the way

31

we'd want it to be, in a *perfect* business world.

No, not "perfect" cleaning, but a level of cleaning fitting our strategy… and that we're not embarrassed or ashamed to "put our name on"!

Second, the contact we worked with from the property management company had to be a reasonable person… *not an insane maniac!*

We mean it. (And we assume if you've been cleaning for any length of time…you know <u>exactly</u> what we mean.)

That's right. We got to a point where we would simply refuse to work for a property manager who could "go off like a bomb" at any time, without warning, and for nearly any reason at all.

No amount of money's worth it.

Lord knows, we learned this painful lesson more times than we care to admit… and we're now more convinced than ever, that no matter how much you try…you simply cannot make some people happy.

We frankly think, they either don't know <u>how</u> to be happy, or simply don't <u>want</u> to! *It's probably the stress*…but whatever it is, we're getting off the topic, which was TERMS.

We were talking about under what terms we might've been willing to clean for a property manager. We've already explained we need to be able to deliver quality cleaning and have a reasonable person as our contact.

The third and fourth terms related to <u>price</u>.

Third, our price had to make us a fair profit, and

Fourth, our price had to give us enough time (avg. nightly hours) to <u>consistently</u> deliver the level of cleaning we promised.

That's it - those were our four terms, or conditions, and, we weren't trying to be *difficult*. But we knew, if we ever wanted to enjoy steady growth, we needed every account to be <u>profitable</u>, <u>stable</u> and <u>clean</u>!

Did you get that? It's important! Here it is again:

If we wanted to enjoy steady growth, then our accounts had to be... **profitable, stable and clean.**

Now, if you can find a property manager to work with where you can meet these terms... you may have found a real winner.

In fact, the up-side is, if you do, most property managers have several, or possibly many buildings for you to bid on. And, if all the stars line up just right... it could be a very sweet deal for you.

However, here's just a final word or two of <u>caution</u>:

First, be careful you don't confuse simply having lots of accounts you clean for a property manager - *with being profitable!*

Second, be careful not to, as the saying goes, "put all your eggs in one basket."

If everything you do is tied to one property manager, you run the risk of getting *squashed* if the "big elephant" you're in bed with ever decides to suddenly roll over... right on top of you!

Now, let's look at **owner-occupied** buildings.

It's probably obvious, but worth saying, that these are buildings where the owner of the building actually uses or occupies some, or all, of the building... to run their <u>own</u> company.

And <u>that</u> difference makes a <u>big</u> difference... when it comes to cleaning.

As you can imagine, the owner of a building who actually uses the building to run their own business generally takes a great deal of pride in the daily appearance of his or her building.

This isn't just some passive "investment" to them, but rather something that tells their employees, customers and the entire community a lot about them - *good or bad*.

So, what may have been quickly dismissed as "too much to spend on cleaning" by a property manager, may be approved relatively easily, in the case of an owner-occupied building who wants their building to "say something wonderful" about the kind of person they are, and the kind of business they run.

They want the cleanliness of the building to say...

1. "This guy runs a tight ship!"

2. "This guy shows an attention to detail."

3. "This guy has a commitment to quality."

Bottom line: Owner-occupied buildings are seen as a reflection of the owner. And, the real connection between *price* and *quality* is generally more **understood** and **accepted** among owners who occupy, than managers, who well…manage.

So, what's the verdict with Owner-occupied buildings?

Yeah, we liked them a lot. And we didn't take them for granted, and suggest you don't either.

They really are gems - An account where the owner is willing to pay for the kind of quality cleaning both of you can be proud of.

4. REGULAR Is Better!

If we had to choose between a <u>regular</u> customer and a <u>one-time</u> or periodic job, we'd take the regular customer, every time!

You might want to do the same. *Here's why.*

Let's say we had the chance to pick between a one time strip/wax job where we could make a <u>whopping</u> **$400 profit in one night**, or a regular office-cleaning contract where we only made **$145 a month**.

Yeah, we'd still take the regular, office-cleaning job - every time!

Why?

Well, every account takes work to get started; all the 'stuff' that has to happen before the job even starts.

There's arranging to see the building, getting the keys, learning the alarms, lining up and training the people to clean etc. But, while it varies a little, it's in many ways basically the <u>same</u> work to get ready.

The difference is in <u>how</u> <u>often</u> you get rewarded for all that up-front work.

With a *one-time* job, you get rewarded as the name implies, just <u>once</u>, or only periodically, while with a *regular* monthly customer, you get **rewarded <u>every</u> <u>month</u> … like clockwork.**

And even though the $400 you could make on the *one-time* job sounds great <u>at first</u>, in less than 3 months, you'd have made <u>even more</u> than that at the *regular* monthly job. ($145/mo. x 3 months = $435 total)

And from then on, it's *smooth sailing*, as the regular job, continues to churn out profits every month, leaving the one-time job... behind in the dust!

Oh, and one other thing…

Who's more likely to "stiff you" when it comes to getting paid:

Your regular office cleaning customer who knows you're coming back again tomorrow night… or the guy you just did a one-time floor job for who may never call or see you again?

You know who.

5. Use LEVERAGE!

For a long time, we were afraid to take on bigger jobs.

We had gotten use to cleaning buildings for $250 to $500/month. The profit <u>margins</u> on the jobs were good and we knew how to take care of them.

So, we were satisfied just trying to get as many of them as we could. We thought by getting a lot of these smaller accounts, at least all of our eggs weren't in one basket.

There was some truth in that, and frankly, there <u>were</u> a lot of jobs in that price range.

But, after a while, we began to realize that starting a bigger job, say a large $1,500 - $4,500/ mo. job was NOT much more trouble than starting a smaller $250 - $500/mo. job.

It didn't take much more, at least not proportionately more, marketing, selling or management time.

And, we began to also understand that while the **profit <u>percentage</u>** (%) on the smaller job was usually much higher than the bigger one, the total **profit <u>dollars</u>** ($) coming in from the bigger account was usually greater, and, well worth any additional work.

Bottom line: We could **leverage** about the same amount of marketing, selling, administrative and management "work"... but get rewarded with more, sometimes significantly more, PROFIT DOLLARS.

In fact, to our surprise, sometimes it was actually _easier_ to manage the larger account.

How can _that_ be?

Well, bigger jobs allowed us to offer our cleaners "better", more stable jobs. For example, we might be able to give two people a more desirable 3½ hr. cleaning shift three nights per week at a bigger job, **versus** just one person, a _less_ desirable 2 hr. shift once a week at the smaller job.

So, our turnover was generally lower at the bigger accounts.

And, keeping turnover down helped keep quality up. (Nothing can wreak havoc on how a building looks more than having new people coming and going all the time.)

Did you catch that? Better shifts with better hours can equal:

- Easier hiring

- Lower turnover

- Higher quality

- Increased stability

And, when your accounts are _clean and stable_, you'll have more time to go out and get more of them!

So, look at "casting your marketing net" a little deeper to where the bigger "fish" swim. The bigger "fish" may be just about as easy to catch, while giving you a whole lot more to "eat".

The next powerful tip is along the same lines as "using leverage" and has to do with how to handle "intimidating" buildings.

6. Don't Be INTIMIDATED

Whether it's a high rise corporate facility downtown or a sprawling medical building in the suburbs, at first, those big buildings can be "intimidating" and scary to think about bidding on.

But here's something to think about.

Sometimes, some of the most "intimidating" buildings can actually be easier than the much smaller ones you already feel comfortable bidding on and cleaning now. (Remember Leverage).

Here's the story...

Years ago, we had a morning meeting with an attorney at a big downtown office building. In fact, it was one of the largest buildings in the area, period.

We got to the meeting a little early, so we took a few minutes to sit down in the main lobby. It was very nice.

Very nice and very quiet

And as we looked around, we began to realize there wasn't another soul around... anywhere. So, we got up to take a closer look.

We walked all over, including down the escalator to where there was a set of restrooms, as well as over near the sets of elevators. We looked everywhere.

And what we discovered was - there was hardly anyone, anywhere to be found. That's right, other than the security guard stationed at the lobby desk; in the large common areas... it was basically <u>empty</u>.

And so, it didn't take us long to realize why the first floor areas looked perfectly clean. It also began to occur to us, that if <u>this</u> is how busy it is at prime time...10:30 in the morning, then it probably doesn't look much different at 5 PM when the tenants head home for the night.

Fine, you may say, but "What about the tenant areas?" If it's a large building, those leased office spaces "may be pretty dirty by the end of the day."

Well, let's put it this way.... from the looks of the few professional and well-mannered attorneys and assistants that slowly and quietly came in to work... we felt we were pretty safe in assuming "they were probably not too rough on the place!" (It certainly wasn't as challenging as, for example, a manufacturing environment.)

Standard dusting, vacuuming, etc? Sure. But, overall, not too bad; nothing we couldn't handle.

It's interesting. Some of the easiest places to clean were our biggest buildings.

How can that be? Well, take a minute to step back and look at it.

Think about how hard you have to work to take a <u>smaller</u>, less intimidating, but a <u>lot</u> filthier building from "dirty" to "clean" overnight - every night!

And, now compare that to keeping a larger, but in some ways easier building, clean. More hours? Sure; *but, proportionally less effort.*

Oh, and by the way...

Do you think it's easier or harder to keep cleaning associates trained and happy in a smaller, dirty building, that's cleaned once a week, or in one that's larger, but easier to maintain, that's cleaned nightly?

And while the <u>percent</u> of profit may not be as high as on the smaller building, the absolute, total, real dollars coming from the bigger building can "dwarf" the profit dollars being generated from smaller facilities.

Important:

If you're just starting out it can be a good idea to begin with smaller buildings to get "your feet wet" by learning the basics of cleaning and managing cleaning.

It can also be a good strategy to take on bigger buildings in "stages"; for example, starting with 2,500 – 10,000 sq. ft. jobs at first, before taking on let's say, 10,000 – 25,000 sq. ft., and then eventually 25,000 – 75,000 sq. ft. buildings and so on.

The time table is really up to you.

But once you're confident of your abilities to hire for and manage the cleaning of buildings… fight the tempting 'knee-jerk' reaction of being scared off by larger buildings.

Instead, take the time to learn about the building and run the numbers to decide if you have, or can afford to get, the resources (know how, managers, equipment, etc.) needed to clean the building.

7. Best Place to Find MORE Business

We hear it all the time.

Cleaning companies of various sizes call our office every day. And what do you think is the one thing they nearly all ask?

Well, if you guessed, "Where can I find more jobs!" then *ding, ding, ding*...you're a winner! That's right; nearly everyone wants <u>more</u> work, more jobs, basically more business.

It's understandable.

But here's the thing...the first and best place to look for <u>more</u> business is right there under your feet, with the businesses you <u>already</u> clean.

Russell Conwell, who wrote the speech titled, *"Acres of Diamonds"*, explains how people tend to look for opportunities nearly everywhere but the <u>one</u> place they're most likely to find it, which is... *in their own backyard!*

That's right, the customers you already have, the businesses you already clean, can be your BEST source of NEW business.

What kind of business?

*   Well, do you provide tile maintenance, exterior window cleaning, carpet or upholstery cleaning or wall washing?

When's the last time you offered any or all of these "extra" services to your own, current customers?

*   How about providing consumable poly/paper products, like toilet tissue, hand towels, hand soap, or trash liners?

When's the last time you offered to take over the "hassle" of inventorying, ordering, tracking, and stocking these supply items for your own, current customers?

It's fine to look down the street for <u>new</u> accounts. *It's fun and exciting.*

But selling more services to your current accounts not only increases your overall sales, the same as new accounts do, but <u>also</u> has the added benefit of creating a stronger bond between you and your current customers.

In sales, we have to show prospective clients they can TRUST us.

Sometimes, that's not easy; especially if they've been let down, or disappointed by janitorial cleaning companies in the past; which is why your own current list of customers is so valuable.

They should <u>already</u> trust you.

Hopefully, they've seen how you and your people can be counted on to deliver quality cleaning. *And that's half the battle*, because people need to trust you... <u>before</u> they are willing to BUY from you.

And brand new accounts aren't any easier than current jobs, in fact, they're harder in some ways. i.e. new equipment, finding and training new people etc.

Brand new accounts are great, but like the old saying goes "The grass may be greener on the other side... *but it still needs to be mowed!"*

So, here's a short list of ways you can develop NEW business from your <u>current</u> customers:

1. **Offer** more services…and promote them more frequently.

2. **Communicate** regularly with your customers about current industry trends like "green" cleaning, "sustainability", or new advances in cleaning equipment etc.

3. **Create** a VIP Customer Focus Group, and ask them for their input, ideas, etc. Show them you appreciate their ideas and for participating in the group. And, of course, find out what they want…and then a way to give it to them!

4. **Survey** your customers to find out what they like and don't like

about your service, as well as what else they want and would buy from you.

Now, let's talk about what you should look for when you're getting ready to go after brand new accounts.

8. MORE Like Your 10 Best

When going after NEW business, it can be useful to follow this simple yet powerful advice…

Try to find more <u>new</u> customers like your 10 *best* <u>current</u> customers. What do we mean by BEST?

Well, by "best" we mean the accounts that always seem to:

1. Run SMOOTHLY - think of easy to staff and manage.

2. Have HAPPY customers – generate few complaints, are very satisfied with your work and may even be willing to act as a reference.

3. Generate LOTS of extra work, but FEW headaches – additional services can be profitable and help build relationships.

You know the "ones"; they seem to be in that perfect "burn zone". If you have 10 of them – great! If you only have 3, or 4 or 5, that's fine too.

The idea is, if you can find out what these "BEST" accounts have in common… you can target more just like them.

Or at least, close.

Here's an example, let's say, in looking at your very best accounts, you find they're nearly all manufacturing facilities, in small nearby towns or cities, requiring a minimum of 5 times per week service.

Well, you may decide to get a targeted list of all of the industrial and manufacturing businesses within an hour of your office... and make them your main target, or at least one of the most important targets of your marketing program.

Or, let's say, you find your best accounts seem to consistently be professional office buildings located at or near downtown, are between 10,000 and 75,000 square feet, and are very conscious of, and value "green", environmentally-friendly cleaning products and methods.

Well, then the same logic applies.

Begin to TARGET accounts like your 10 BEST, and you may quickly find you're cleaning business is not only more profitable but easier to run. And that, as Martha Stewart would say, is a good thing!

Next, let's look at the importance of precise target marketing.

9. AIM Small Miss Small

In the movie, *The Patriot*, Mel Gibson in his role as a revolutionary war patriot, asks his young sons if they remember what he taught them about using a rifle and the key to good marksmanship.

They do, and quickly answer together, *"Aim small, miss small!"*

They knew if they wanted to improve their chances of hitting the target, they needed to narrow down their view, and focus their attention.

The <u>same</u> thing is true for hitting <u>any</u> target.

You want to focus. You want to create a very select group of targeted companies to go after.

Your target list may consist of 50 or 500 potential prospects; a lot depends on the kind of accounts you want.

If you're going after construction clean-up work within 50 miles of your office, you may have a list of only 25 general contractors you want to direct your marketing efforts towards.

If you're looking to do residential cleaning, you may have hundreds or thousands of homes that fall into your targeted service area with the demographics you're looking for.

As we've mentioned, our niche service was providing general office cleaning and related services, three to five nights per week in the early evening to professional, industrial, and manufacturing facilities within 50 miles of our office.

Then, we <u>narrowed</u> down our list even further.

We determined our <u>very best</u> accounts would be professional, industrial and manufacturing companies that had between 25-150 employees.

Why 25 -150 employees?

Because those were the companies that generally had enough employees to warrant hiring a cleaning service... but not so many they simply handled the cleaning themselves using their own in-house staff.

Interestingly, a lot has changed in recent years.

Now, with the increased trend towards outsourcing...even companies with 250 or more employees would have been good prospects for us.

Anyway, back to the story…

We used a business database company to find out who met our guidelines and came up with a list of about 375 companies that "fit the bill".

This was <u>our</u> target - the companies we'd direct all of our marketing efforts towards. You can do the same thing.

Find out what your absolutely best accounts would look like and then **make a targeted list** of them. But, how do you do that?

Let's tackle that now.

10. Top 5 BEST Lists

How can you put together a target list? Here are five of the best:

1. A list of businesses you buy through an online service based on factors such as size, employee account, location etc.

2. A list you put together yourself by continually spotting, verifying and adding new buildings that meet your target profile.

3. An **"endorsed" list** where another service provider (i.e. uniform/floor mat cleaning company, coffee service, security service, lawn care service etc.) gives you permission to send a letter to <u>their</u> business customers with their endorsement.

4. A list built by **companies "opting in" online**; responding to an offer of a FREE report on, for example, the "Top 10 Mistakes People Make When Hiring A New Cleaning Company!

5. Your **own customer list**. Don't be surprised. Your customers, and the referrals they give you, can be an incredible source of future business.

11. Make S.M.A.R.T Calls!

So, what do you do once you have a list of targeted companies that fit your niche or target market requirements?

You make S.M.A.R.T calls.

You may be wondering, "What are those?"

Well, "S.M.A.R.T" calls are phone calls you make to learn specific facts about every prospect on your list.

Here's what a S.M.A.R.T call is about:

S - Speak calmly; keep it light . No need for high pressure selling here.

M - Make notes, changes and updates to basic information like company name, address and phone number.

A - Ask for the NAME of the person in charge of hiring the cleaning company - the decision maker. And, YES, spelling counts!

R - Remember to listen for other information; for example, how often they are being cleaned now, who's doing it, and when.

T - Thanks! -"Thanks, that's all I needed!" Again, keep it light.

Here's how a S.M.A.R.T call might sound:

* * * ring, ring, ring * * *

Them: Hello, Acme Manufacturing, How can I direct your call.

You: Oh, yes, thank you, this is John Smith from ABC Cleaning, and I'm trying to send a brochure to the person there at Acme Mfg. in charge of hiring the office-cleaning company. Who do you think I should send that to?

Them: *Oh, I don't know for sure, probably Ted Stevens the Plant Manager. But, I know they already have a service that comes in three nights a week.*

You: Oh, no problem, that's fine, I just want to send something in the mail to him he might like to keep in his files. I see you've changed your name to Acme Manufacturing?

Them: *Yes, it was Acme Widgets, but it changed recently.*

You: Right, and are you still on Opportunity Drive?

Them: *Yes.*

You: Ok, great, that's all I needed; Thanks for your help!

****

Now, LOOK what you've learned:

1. Their <u>NEW company name</u>,

2. That they already have a cleaning contractor, so you know they use contract cleaning, rather than having it done in-house.

3. That the cleaning is done <u>at night</u>.

4. That the cleaning is done <u>3x/ week</u>.

5. The <u>NAME of the decision maker</u>!

Using the S.M.A.R.T call method, you can confirm at least two things:

A. Whether or not they should be included in your targeted list, and

B. If so, the name of the person you'll want to direct your ongoing marketing to.

And, *that's it*, unless...

-You're happen to be talking directly to the actual decision maker, in which case, you might say, "Well that's all I needed; I'll make sure you get our brochure, unless you'd like a free estimate for your files now."

Or

-You're speaking to the receptionist and he/she mentions that he/she knows that they are unhappy with their cleaning, and offers to put you right through to the decision maker.

Remember:

-Keep your S.M.A.R.T calls *slow and easy*; you <u>don't</u> have to worry about hard-selling anybody. If you keep it "low or no-pressure" generally so will the person on the other end of the phone.

-S.M.A.R.T calls are the way to get your target list of prospects ready to mail for <u>maximum results</u>!

-And S.M.A.R.T calls save you tons of time and money by getting your message to the right person the first time!

INSIDER SECRET # 2
Use Measurable Guarantees of Performance

12. REINVENT Your Business…before it's too late!

Scary, we know, but let's be honest - today isn't like yesterday.

Yesterday, you might have been able to "pick and choose" which accounts you wanted….

Today, you're just downright grateful for <u>every</u> customer you have and every building you clean!

Yesterday, you could expect to see at least a few decent applicants apply to work for you…..

Today, you wonder if there's <u>anyone</u> out there even <u>willing</u> to work anymore, or at least anyone you'd <u>want</u> working for you!

Yesterday, you could at least go out and land jobs where you'd have <u>enough</u> <u>hours</u> to clean the way you'd like, and deliver the kind of quality you like to give....

Today, you question whether or not anyone even <u>cares</u> what the actual cleaning will be like as you watch your prospects skip everything else... *and go right to the price page!*

Yesterday, you could count on your "contacts", who've gotten to be friends of yours over the years, to always be there...

Today, the building and property manager contacts you've developed over the years can <u>disappear</u> in a "puff of smoke" as your friend is suddenly transferred, reassigned or has his or her position eliminated altogether, leaving you standing there like the nervous new kid at school, wondering who to sit next to at lunch. Ugh!

We could go on, but we won't, because the point is clear - Today isn't yesterday.

Harder? Sure, but <u>not</u> impossible.

And, we're sorry, *but here's some more bad news.....*

13. Being "GREEN" Isn't Going To Save You

It's a constant drumbeat.

Frankly, it's just about the <u>only</u> thing you hear anymore! *You know what we're talking about...*

Green Cleaning!

Yep, cleaning companies are "climbing all over each other" so they don't miss out on announcing to the world... "We're GREEN!"

It's said a million different ways...

- "We offer GREEN cleaning!"

- "We're GREEN cleaning specialists!"

- "We use only GREEN products!"

- "We follow only GREEN cleaning procedures and methods!"

Great, *we get it*, you're "green", but, what <u>else</u> are you?

<u>Don't get us wrong</u>. We're <u>not</u> criticizing the push towards the use of environmentally-friendly "green" products and practices. Indoor air pollution is a serious issue, and the use of "green" products and methods of cleaning promises to go a long way in tackling the problem.

So, we're <u>not</u> lookin' for a fight! We're just here to say…

…If you think getting on the "green" train is going to be your ticket to fame and fortune in the cleaning business ... *better think again!*

That's right, just being "green" <u>isn't</u> going to cut it!

It's just NOT going to be enough.

How can we say that?! It's nearly all you read about anymore, isn't it? - how environmentally friendly, "green" products and methods are the answer to nearly <u>everything</u> you need to know about the cleaning business.

Case closed. *Right?*

Well, maybe... maybe not. Let us explain.

If you're asking us if the use of these "green" products and methods are going to be an essential part of what any professional cleaning company offers their customers and trains their employees on... <u>then YES, absolutely</u>!

In fact, we would go so far as to say, in the not too distant future... we could see it becoming a virtual "requirement" of what may soon be considered "standard" janitorial office-cleaning.

So, yeah, we think it's important.

But, if you're asking us if "green cleaning" is going to be the only ticket you need to grow a fast growing and profitable cleaning company... then, we've got to say NO, not by a long shot!

But, boy, it would be great if it could.

Really, wouldn't it be great if all you had to do was find out about "green" products, train your people on "green" methods, and then announce to all your prospective clients that you were now.. GREEN ... and they'd come flocking to you in droves begging YOU to clean their building... Ahhhh... that would be a sweet dream...

But that's all it is.... a dream.

And, if you're honest with yourself, and think about it carefully, you know, nothing's <u>that</u> easy. Nothing of value, nothing you can count on. Nothing that lasts.

No, the truth is...if the future is going to force everyone...the willing, and unwilling, to "get on board" the "green" train... well, then in a short time, guess what?

That's right, everyone, or nearly <u>everyone</u>, will be using affordable and readily available "green" products and having their people following easy-to-learn "green" methods.

And, then... how 'special" will any <u>one</u> of them be more than another... if they're <u>all</u> "green"?

That's right, not very!

So, if just being "green" isn't going to give you the competitive edge, what will? We'll talk about that next.

For now, just know that there is a way out of all this doom and gloom, and here's how it starts.....

14. Give 'Em What They WANT

Ok, we'll just go ahead and tell you.

Here's what you absolutely must know about your customers if you want to explode your sales and profits:

What they WANT and NOT what you think they need.

See, the business *grave yard* is filled with failed companies that tried in vain to sell what they *thought* their customers needed... rather than what the customers *said* they wanted.

That's right, know-it-all business owners are digging their own graves when they get it in their head that customers will buy anything they try to sell them.

So, instead, ask your customers what they want. It's simple, but it can be something we resist doing.

Why?

Oh, probably lots of reasons.

Well, laziness, of course, which is the root of many of our problems. But, there are other reasons.

For example, you may think you already know what the customers want. But do you?

Let's say, for example, you put together a cleaning proposal offering fewer days of service because you knew they wanted to save money, and

<u>you thought</u> that was the best way to get the savings. When delivering the proposal, however, you find out <u>what they actually wanted</u> was to save the money NOT by getting fewer days of service, but rather by having their own people take care of a few cleaning tasks themselves. Oops, is right!

Another reason we resist asking our customers is embarrassment.

We may think (incorrectly of course) the customer will think less of us if we have to ask them what they want. We may feel we should already know what they need without asking. *Right?*

No way, in fact, the opposite is generally true.

Think about it. Don't you like it when someone asks YOU what you're looking for from a product or service? Of course you do! And <u>your</u> customers are no different.

You may want to send out a written survey. You may want to conduct a survey by phone or in person.

Anyway you decide to do it, you're likely to find some surprises about what is, and what is not, important to your customers.

Then, at that point, what does your job become?

Simply this: To solve the problems your customers say they <u>absolutely</u> have to have solved....and consistently give them the "things" they said they <u>absolutely</u> have to get from their cleaning service?

Exciting? Yes! Easy? No.

But isn't that a goal worth having?

And, just as importantly, wouldn't <u>that</u> be something that could have customers lining up to hire you?...*Thought that would get your attention!*

15. What Do They REALLY Want?

So, what do customers as well as prospects <u>really</u> want?

Well, we'll tell you right now, it's NOT "perfect cleaning".

Why?

Because they know, as well as you, that the idea of "perfect" *anything* is ridiculous at best.

In fact, they know cleaning companies that promise things like "perfect cleaning" or "no mistakes" are kidding themselves or, worse yet, trying to fool them!

That's right, they know better.

They know, after watching an endless parade of cleaning companies (*who promised everything but the moon and the stars),* fall flat on their face.... that "perfect" cleaning is neither perfect... nor possible.

No, instead, they all eventually learned to avoid those promising perfection and start looking for something else instead.

And what is that? What do customers really want from their janitorial cleaning service?

Best price? ... sure, they look at it .. but no, it's <u>not</u> just price.

Well then, what is it?

It's this:

Real answers to their real problems

And what exactly are their real problems?

Well, ask a hundred companies and you'll get a hundred different

57

answers. But you'll find <u>some</u> things said over and over again; common things they're looking for.

Let's *listen* to them. Isn't this what they're <u>really</u> saying:

"We want a cleaning service that...

1. <u>Knows</u> our building,

2. <u>Understands</u> what we need,

3. <u>Has a specific plan</u> to consistently deliver the cleaning we need at a price we can justify (notice; we didn't say lowest),

4. <u>Has a track record</u> to show they can do it and, finally,...

5. <u>Is willing to guarantee it!</u>"

Let's break this down to see what we can learn...

They want you to <u>know</u> their building & what they want. **Do you?**

Does your proposal and presentation prove that you know the ins and outs of their building? Does your proposal and presentation prove you've listened to them and "get" what they want? (CUSTOMIZED)

They want you to <u>have</u> the right plan. **Do you?**

Does your proposal and presentation clearly describe the steps to your plan, the people who'll implement the plan, and the systems to make sure it works! (PLAN, SYSTEMS)

They want you to <u>offer</u> a price they can justify. **Can you?**

Does your proposal and presentation clearly show how you arrived at your price and how it is tied directly to the level of service and supervision they need? (VALUE)

They want you to <u>prove</u> you can deliver consistently! **Can you?**

Does your proposal and presentation offer a strong, specific guarantee of performance backed by a proven track record to show you can deliver? (GUARANTEE)

So, <u>what do you do</u> once you find out what they really WANT? Let's look at that next.

16. Measurable Guarantee of Performance (MGP)

As buyers, we're all the same.

We're looking for someone who can show they have <u>real answers</u> to our <u>real problems</u>....*and be willing to guarantee it!*

We call these real answers MGPs, or **Measurable Guarantees of Performance.**

Over the years, we've read a number of other marketers explain similar concepts called USP's, which stands for Unique Selling Propositions or UCA's, which stands for Unique Competitive Advantages.

But, we prefer our term, MGP, for a couple **important** reasons:

1. MGPs emphasize the importance of MEASUREMENT. Anyone can make broad claims. Measurable ones are more difficult to create, let alone guarantee. But that's why they're so much more powerful and effective.

2. MGPs emphasize the importance of GUARANTEE. This speaks for itself. You say you'll do something, but will you stand behind it...financially!

3. MGPs emphasize the importance of PERFORMANCE. And in the cleaning business that's what it's all about – service performance.

Here's an example of an MGP dealing with the important topic of quality:

Our Quality Guarantee:

"You'll Be 100% Delighted With The Quality Of Each Cleaning Visit… or it's FREE" *

* *To guarantee you get the quality of cleaning you deserve, your building will be thoroughly inspected using our special nightly "QC Check System", which will be graded, faxed to our office and placed on your desk. If you disagree with a daily "grade", or feel you were not cleaned properly on any visit… it's FREE!*

Bold?…*Yes!*

Hard to create the systems required to support making this kind of strong statement and guarantee? … *Absolutely!*

But think about this for a minute…

How different would your company be if you could offer a set of 5 or more of these MGPs hitting on every single one of the most important "answers" your prospects are desperately looking for?

Yeah, very different.

In fact, we believe developing a set of powerful Measurable Guarantees of Performance may be the single most important thing you can do to quickly move your cleaning business forward.

By the way, if your experience ends up being anything even close to ours…you have little to fear in offering these bold MGPs;

Your worst nightmares of customers lined up to take advantage of your generous guarantees by demanding refunds… are seldom realized.

And an occasional refund having to be paid to a customer, where you did, in fact, "drop the ball" may be a good thing now and again - a 'wake-up' call to keep you "on your toes", force you to re-evaluate your systems and avoid becoming complacent.

Plus, the cost of an occasional refund should be far outweighed by the incredible customer satisfaction, loyalty and referral business resulting from the strong guarantees you promote, and the systems you use to make them possible.

Frankly, we probably didn't have a handful of clients take us up on any of our guarantee offers over our many years in business.

In reality, human nature generally shows that the great majority of customers are not waiting anxiously to "hold your feet to the fire" to demand a refund; on the contrary, most want things to work out between the two of you.

INSIDER SECRET #3
Get Prospects to Ask for You

17. Have SOMETHING to Say

People always complain they can't think of anything <u>new</u>, <u>different</u> or <u>interesting</u> to say in their marketing.

And why is that?

Simply put, they have nothing new, different or interesting to offer.

It's about that simple.

And it's the most <u>common</u> thing in the world, because finding a company willing to think differently and act differently is extremely <u>uncommon</u>.

In an industry where sales calls are made and brochures are sent out with no more exciting a message than "free estimates, bonded and insured... call today"...it's easy for the prospect to feel uninspired...*or downright bored.*

You need to be *different!*

So, rather than follow the masses, you need to strike out on your own, by taking the time to find out what your customers want and the ways to consistently give it to them.

For example...

1. If they're tired of seeing what seems like a "new face" assigned to clean their building each week ...*figure out what practical steps you can take to effectively control your rate of employee turnover.*

2. If they want to be able to reduce the number of contractors they need to call to get various maintenance services performed like carpet cleaning or stocking poly/paper products... *learn how you can offer these services for them, so you can be their one-stop shop!*

3. If they are worried about security in their building ... *create a series of procedures to tighten up the your level of protection in all area of your cleaning business, such as protecting keys and codes, screening of applicants, or requiring your staff to wear uniforms and ID badges.*

It's up to <u>you</u> to find out what your customers want and to create ways to make sure they get it.

Do <u>that,</u> and you will have something new, different and interesting to say in your marketing.

Now, as we promised, we're not going to pull any punches. This process of creating these steps, procedures and systems isn't easy, not by a long shot.

Most people won't even try to do it... and even fewer will follow it through to the end. The great majority of people today seem perfectly willing to do nothing at all, content to have *lowest price* be their "competitive advantage".

But isn't something very wrong when your company's claim-to-fame is you're simply willing to do the work for less than the next guy?

We sure as heck think so, and hope you think so too.

How sad to have to say, "We're a great cleaning company because we're <u>really</u> cheap."

And that, friend, is a strategy that will only last until they find someone willing to do it at an even lower price..

<u>It doesn't have to be that way... not for you!</u>

Bottom line:

You can find ways, create systems and implement procedures that can be counted on to consistently deliver what your customers WANT.

Then, you can create Measurable Guarantees of Performance to highlight how you're uniquely able to guarantee you can solve your customer's most pressing problems.

Then, you can use an on-going sequential marketing plan to consistently show your customers the BENEFITS your one-of-a-kind MGPs can deliver to them... Guaranteed!

18. Get FILED To Get Hired

That's an insider tip you'll want to remember.

Specifically, you want to get your company info. i.e. sales letter, brochures etc. into your prospect's file: the one they keep in their office drawer about cleaning.

Oh, and we're not talking about sneaking into their office in the middle of the night to do it. (Hint; sending a great direct response sales letter by mail will do just fine... more about that later.)

Anyway, more about this very important file in just a moment...

First, let's review;

We've talked about how we want to "Aim to Be Next", so the prospect immediately thinks of calling us, and only us, if the current contractor drops the ball, or the client simply goes out to bid.

Well, now, we want to look at one of the most powerful ways to do just that. And it's by getting our information into our prospect's file on CLEANING.

Why is that so important?

Well, over the years, we've discovered something very interesting about the person in charge of hiring the cleaning company.

It doesn't seem to matter if it's an office manager, maintenance supervisor, facilities manager or President of the company... they almost always have a file in their office labeled "CLEANING" or "JANITORIAL SERVICES".

But why in the world would we want to have our company info just sitting in a file drawer, gathering dust?

Simple...

Because it is very often THAT file they pull out when they get ready to change contractors. And it is THAT file where they put the brochures, business cards and sales letters of the cleaning companies they will choose from.

But don't we want to get hired NOW, not later?

Sure, we all love it when we send a sales letter, or make a call, and almost immediately get an interested prospect.

It sometimes happens. And when it does, it's great!

But our experience is that many times, maybe 8 out of 10 times, a prospect isn't ready to change services right away. They may want to in the future, maybe even soon, but not just yet.

So, we want them to remember us, and think of us, as the next company they will turn to when that time comes.

<u>Getting our company in their mind, and in that file, is one great way to do just that!</u>

19. Call OR Send?

Should you call your prospect or send them something.

It's an important question. And the answer is... well, both, but in our strategy, we do each for very different reasons.

Call?

Yes, we suggest calling (remember S.M.A.R.T calls), but primarily to identify the name of the person who is the decision maker - the one who hires the cleaning contractor. But, in general...

We don't sell on calls, we IDENTIFY.

Why?

Well, because personal calling sounds great, at first. And when it *occasionally* works, it's exciting. But our experience tells us, that it's generally too time consuming, expensive and ineffective.

Some of the problems include:

1. It's often hard, if not impossible, to catch people in. Most, if not nearly all the time, your call is screened or put through to voice mail.

2. Many business people are so busy, or stressed out, you can sense it right away; they may feel suspicious, or "put out" by your sales pitch. And remember, while people <u>do</u> like to buy, they don't like to be sold! So, we want to attract them… not hound them!

3. The painful rejection of cold calling makes it hard, if not impossible, to stick to a strict discipline of scheduled calls.

Or, think of it this way; which approach do you think works best:

A. Where someone has "talked them into" allowing you to bid their building, or

B. Where someone likes what they've learned about you through your marketing so much that they - <u>call</u> to <u>ask</u> for <u>YOU</u> to come out?

Now, to be fair, we do make a few exceptions to this no-telemarketing "rule":

First, if, during the initial survey call we refer to as a "S.M.A.R.T" call, the person on the line comes right out, says they're interested, and directly asks for a bid; we'll go into sales mode and set up the walk-through.

Second; when the call is simply one step in a long series of scheduled steps in a marketing sequence, it can be handled as a sales call as well.

But these exceptions are mostly that, exceptions.

So, what about SEND?

Yes, we strongly do suggest sending regular mailings i.e. sales letters, brochures, mailers, reports, etc. to your prospects as a great strategy to GROW!

Not one mailing. Not a mailing because things are slow.

No, we're talking about a series of powerful marketing pieces lined up and ready to be sent out on a REGULAR basis to each prospect on your target list following a pre-determined schedule!

The marketing POWER comes from the powerful marketing pieces going out on a scheduled basis. And, that's a strategy to grow every month, not just this month!

20. Every SIX Weeks!

Prospects are like kids... they just don't get it the first time.

You know how kids can be. Tell them to clean up their room. No response.

Tell them again, still no response.

After a series of more and more powerful directives ... and they <u>might</u> begin to move.

Prospects can be like that.

You dangle highly desirable marketing "bait" in front of your prospects eyes, but they don't all rush to "bite" at it.

It'd be nice if they did... *but they generally don't!*

Why not?

Well, because prospects very often need to see your message over and over again, before they're willing to take the "plunge" (i.e. call, order, buy).

Savvy marketers know it takes multiple "touches" or marketing communications from you, before prospects are ready to act. Some say, 5, 6, 7 or more.

At one time, we had in place a series of 20 marketing steps or "touches" (direct response letters, brochures, postcards, scheduled calls, etc.) which we would generally send out, one at a time, over the course of about 18 months; each going out about six to seven weeks apart.

We also had a couple sets of 3-step series letters in there... we'll talk about that shortly. But, whatever the number of "touches" it takes to get prospects to respond -

It's safe to say, it isn't very often - one.

The point is clear: Having a series of regularly scheduled "touches" or marketing steps in place to repeatedly tell your story... is the key!

And one big advantage of lining up a series of pre-scheduled marketing steps helps to create an ONGOING and STEADY stream of new customers ...rather than "feast or famine".

And, this is BIG.

Sure, it takes some time to put the sequential marketing steps in place; direct response letters, 3-step series mailings, calls, unusual marketing mailings, seasonal pieces.

But, when you do have them in place, you have a powerful, nearly automatic marketing machine to keep YOU in the minds of your prospects.

Some call it "top of mind" awareness. Whatever you want to call it... it's a smart and effective way to position your cleaning business to grow.

So, how often is often enough?

Short answer - Your prospects should hear from you or get <u>something</u> from you about every six weeks!

But remember, it can take many forms.

It can be a sales letter, telemarketing calls, marketing mailer, special report, or brochure. But, the point is to get your company's powerful marketing messages (i.e. MGPs) in front of your prospect about EVERY (6) SIX WEEKS.

Why Six Weeks?

Well, because every six weeks comes across as a *gentle reminder*; not too often that it's seen as a nuisance, and not too little that it's forgotten.

Every six weeks is like what the "Baby Bear" said about his porridge, "Mmmm...just right!"

21. How Many BROCHURES Should We Mail?

We understand why people are always asking how many brochures to send out. We really do.

But the question of whether to send out 100 brochures a week or 100 brochures a month, well, that just...

isn't the <u>right</u> question.

First, of course, it isn't just brochures you should be sending, but rather a series of powerful, direct response marketing pieces. But, for now, to keep things simple, we'll talk in terms of brochures.

Second, the right question, or at least, the better question, isn't really <u>one</u> question at all, but rather a **series** of several questions. Here are a few of the most important ones:

1. What is our monthly sales goal?

2. What is the average monthly price of the jobs we bid on?

3. How many marketing pieces such as sales letters or brochures do we usually have to send out to get a request for bid?

4. How many of those bids turn into new accounts?

Can you see how simply asking how many marketing pieces to send out is essentially "putting the cart before the horse"?

Instead, try this...

Start with a sales goal <u>first</u>, and then work your way *backwards* to figure out how many accounts you'll need on average to:

- reach your sales goal, and

- based on experience, how many bids you'll need to submit to land that many accounts, and

- based on experience, how many letters or brochures you'll need to send out to get the necessary number of requests for bids

Now, <u>that's</u> a better way of coming up with a strategy that will get you where you want to go! Let's look at an example...

Let's say, for example, we wanted to add on about $3000/mo. in new business.

By watching the response to our marketing, we might learn that it takes 50 marketing pieces per week to get 3 bid requests per week, which produce 4 new accounts per month, which add up to a total of approx.$2,500 - $3,500/ mo. in new business.

So, we might start by sending 50 pieces per week as a strategy to get us to our monthly sales goal.

Plans have to be "watched over", and this is no exception.

If you find your strategy isn't producing sufficient requests for bids to get you to your goal, or too many requests for you to keep up with, you always need to be prepared to make adjustments

But you're better off making a few minor course corrections to a well thought out plan, rather than big overhaul-like changes to a strategy that wasn't thought out well, or at all, in the first place.

22. Credibility AND Believability

We've talked about the importance of sending something to our prospects every 6 weeks.

Now, let's talk about what that something should be? Well, here are definitely two of them:

Credibility and *Believability*.

Think about yourself. What do you look for when you're going to hire a service tech? plumber? electrician?

First, you might start with wanting to know if the service person is credible? Meaning, are they trained? Certified? Insured? Licensed? Experienced?

Those are some of the things you, or for that matter any of us, look for. Basically, we want to see if they're qualified to handle the job; in other words - CREDIBILITY!

Second, is the service person believable? We want <u>real stories from real people</u>! Testimonials, for example.

Isn't that right?

We want to hear, or read, about real-life experiences from others who have done business with that service person or service company.

That's how we decide if they're BELIEVABLE.

So, what do we want to send?

Well, it should be something showing our company is both - *credible* and *believable.*

Important Note #1: Have you ever noticed how every building owner or property manager seems to have a *horror story* about a cleaning company.

Why do we mention this? ...because based on these negative experiences, proving our credibility and believability may possibly be even MORE important than in other types of service businesses.

Important Note #2 In our line of work, we often have a high level of unsupervised access to nearly all areas of a customer's building. In fact, in some cases, we may be the only service provider trusted to operate alone in the building - after hours!

It's another important reason why proving our credibility and believability is so important to our prospects.

So, how do we actually prove our credibility and believability?

Well, there are various ways. Here's two of the best:

First -Testimonials. The actual endorsement of real customers is 'hands down' hard to beat.

For example, Mr. Joe Smith from XYZ Company says, "ABC Cleaning Company always keeps our offices in tip top shape. We've been using them for 2 ½ yrs. Their staff is reliable. We'd recommend them to anyone looking for quality cleaning!"

In general, the longer and more detailed the testimonial - the better! You'll need to take the time to get their written permission to use their comments, name, company logo, etc. in your marketing, but it's well worth it!

Second - Visual Proof. Another way to create believability is visual proof. An actual photo showing the amazing before-and-after results of a recent carpet or tile job can do wonders to win over your prospect.

Remember: As the saying goes "A picture is worth ...." - well, you know the rest!

23. ONE-Word Secret to Getting Testimonials

We've just explained the vital role testimonials play in building believability in the minds of our prospects, now we have to have an effective way at getting them.

What <u>others</u> say about you is very often much more important to your prospect... than anything you could ever say about yourself!

So, what is the one-word secret to getting testimonials?

Ask!

It's that simple. *It's that difficult.*

It seems easy enough, to ask for a testimonial, but it can be a little unnerving at first.

So, here are a few "habits" that can keep giving you a steady stream of powerful testimonials:

Habit #1: When someone leaves you a message or sends in an email complimenting your cleaning staff, you should make a point of always asking them if they'd be willing to let you use it as a testimonial.

Habit #2: You can ask it this way: "That's very nice of you to say! As you may know, we're trying to grow our business. And we were wondering if you'd be willing to let us use your comments as a testimonial in our marketing?"

Habit #3: You might want to go even further by saying: "Your endorsement may be just what a potential client needs to hear to convince them to... give us a try!"

Then, here's the other tough part:

Habit #4: <u>Wait for their answer.</u>

That's right, it's like asking for a sale, once you've asked don't fill the uncomfortable silence by talking. Let your words sink in.

You'll be surprised how many people will be more than happy to give you what you've asked for. They own, or work in, a business too. They can see how hard you work. And they also know how valuable a quality testimonial can be!

The fact is, many customers when asked are more than willing to act as a reference for you, but, again... you need to ASK.

24. Make 'Em FEEL the Pain

Prospects are people first!

Prospects are people first!

Prospects are people first!

It's something to keep reminding yourself of.

Too many times we make the mistake of thinking prospects are practical businessmen and women, who, when shown your qualifications and long list of reasons to hire you...will quickly come to a logical decision... and take action; namely, hire you.

We all know better than that, *don't' we?*

If people, including prospects, were totally logical, selling would be a breeze.

But it isn't.....is it?

Why? Well, because prospects are <u>people</u> first.

And because they're people first, they very often may need to feel a certain amount of pain....if you're going to get them to take action!

What pain?

Well, since we're talking about selling more cleaning accounts here.... the pain of their current cleaning situation.

That's right! They're going to need to see, and feel, enough "pain" associated with the state of their current cleaning, that they're actually willing to make an effort and do something about it.

And guess whose job it is to get them to see and feel that pain.... yep.... YOURS!

How?

Well, by <u>consistently</u>, <u>dramatically</u>, and sometimes <u>emotionally</u> painting a picture of the painful problems that come from having the wrong cleaning company.

Here's an example of what we're talking about...

Let's say... you have a testimonial from one of your current clients describing how painful it was <u>before</u> hiring you... when they could never get a hold of the cleaning company, even at times when they had a VIP customer coming and desperately needed extra work done.

Your client may go on to tell in financial, and even emotional terms, how **frustrating** it was to not be able to get ready for a VIP visit, how **upsetting** it was to not be able to reach anyone, how **embarrassing** it was when the VIP's arrived to see a mess... and maybe even how financially **disastrous** it was, if it cost them some much-needed business.

What if your prospects heard or read <u>that</u> painful story?

And then, how would it be if that same customer described how fantastic things are, now that they've hired you? "Powerful" is right!

And do you think they might relate to it... and maybe even have experienced something similar a time or two themselves?

When prospects FEEL that pain... they may, finally, be willing to do something about it.

What <u>other</u> potential sources of PAIN to businesses are there relating to cleaning companies' service... or lack thereof?

- *How about when no one shows up to clean?*

- *How about when carpets get ruined because chemicals are improperly marked or not marked at all?*

- *How about when a door to the building is left unlocked overnight? How about when things come up missing?*

- *How about when customers don't know who in the world will be showing up to clean their building from one night to the next because of out-of-control turnover?*

All of these things can be incredibly painful to businesses.

Now, here's the important payoff:

When you consistently, dramatically, even emotionally paint this picture for them in your marketing, THEN, when they hear your answer to fix what's ailing them, you're likely to have their... UNDIVIDED ATTENTION!

25. SERIES Power is Serious Power

Sitting on our receptionist's desk was a business card. It was from an insurance agent who stopped by while we were out of the office.

No big deal.

Oh, *wait a minute*, did we mention, he had written us a personal note in blue ink on his calling card asking:

"Do you have 15 minutes available Thursday, March 5th?"

Well, that was a little different; personal, took a little bit of effort.

We tossed it in a drawer.

Two days later, we walked into our office and listened to a voice mail from that same insurance salesman explaining how he had stopped by a few days ago... to introduce himself and, if possible, set up a 15 minute meeting.

Hmmm... again, *interesting*, but we still just deleted the message.

15 minutes later, we booted up our computers only to find this same insurance salesman had left both of us personalized e-mails...

Here is basically what his email said.... My name is Steve Stevens (not his real name). I am following up on a business card I left for you this past Friday, and a voicemail left moments ago. I would like to set up a brief...etc.

Can you guess what we did?

Yeah... we called this guy.

That's right, we let him come in to give us his pitch. Why?

Perseverance?

Sure, no doubt about it, his persistence showed he was a dedicated pro. But that wasn't all.

No, it was also the power of using a small but closely timed series of marketing steps such as letters, calls, brochures etc. And, for years, successful marketers have been using this technique to maximize their response rates.

Effective? *You bet!*

In fact, if memory serves us, reports about series letters suggest that response rates to Steps 2 and 3 together can often equal the response rate to Step 1, effectively doubling the total response.

For example; Step One: 5%, Step Two: 3%, Step Three: 2%.

Lesson: Don't make the mistake of leaving "money on the table" by not using the power of a series of marketing pieces.

Now, let's take an even closer look at this strategy.

26. Use 3-Step Series Letters to GROW

How might you use a variation of this series technique in your cleaning business?

We learned how to do this from an incredible direct-response marketing expert, Dan Kennedy, who was instrumental in developing and promoting the effective use of 3-step series letters to market products and services.

It breaks our every six weeks "rule", but the effect is worth it. Here's an example of how the technique can work:

Have you ever gotten a marketing letter in the mail and quickly pitched it, only to have another one arrive in your mailbox just 7-10 days later, this time stamped at the top with the cautionary note - **Second Notice!**

Now, to this second notice, you might give slightly more attention, but still end up simply tossing it in the trash; only to receive yet one more letter, again, about 10 days later; only this time stamped clearly with the warning... **Final Notice!**

It gets your attention. It's *human nature*.

In fact, you may even notice it's basically the <u>same</u> ad you got just a week or two ago, but this time, for some reason, you give it <u>more</u> attention than the last time.

You see, it's the repetition of the same powerful marketing message being reinforced with a slightly different headline or wording, <u>within a relatively short period of time,</u> that seems to "force" you to pay more attention.

Let's take a look at how you can use this idea in marketing your cleaning business.

First, you send **Marketing Letter #1**

Then, 10 days later, you send **Marketing Letter #2** to those who haven't responded to Marketing Letter #1.

It can, in fact, look nearly the same as Letter #1, but this time it would be marked as **Second Notice.**

You <u>can</u> include new wording near the top explaining how...

"You were "bothered" or "wondered why" you hadn't heard from them".... because "You know they are <u>exactly</u> the kind of business client who can benefit the <u>most</u> from your unique services."

You may go on to mention, you were "surprised" to see they had not jumped on your "50% OFF Your 1st Month's Bill" offer, or whatever compelling offer you've created.

In either case, 10 days later, you send still another letter, **Marketing Letter #3**, to those who have not responded to either letters #1 or #2.

This third letter can be labeled **Final Notice**, and accompanied by another, but this time, even <u>more urgent</u> plea for your prospect to take action.

Again, it may look and read essentially the same as Marketing Letters #1 and #2, but this time it may have a slightly different headline or wording, such as...

"At first, we were just a little concerned, but now we're downright "worried", because if we don't hear from you soon - very soon, you will have completely missed out on your <u>only</u> chance this year to take advantage of your "50% OFF Your 1st Month's Bill" special!

Make sense?

Three separate, but related, marketing pieces sent out 10 days apart in a pre-set sequence to capture your prospect's attention and motivate them to act.

Putting together one or more of these 3-Step Series marketing programs takes some effort... but doesn't everything that's worthwhile?

27. Show Them the MONEY

But, "What about price?" you may want to ask. "Come on, you know that's all anyone seems to care about! Right?"

Fair question.

Well, price should be <u>much</u> less of an issue once you've "cracked the code" of knowing what your customers WANT and then HOW to get it for them by creating powerful operational systems that consistently deliver it.

And it's <u>those</u> Measurable Guarantees of Performance (MGPs) that you need to communicate regularly to your prospects in your marketing.

It is one of the best ways to move the conversation from PRICE to

VALUE. In other words, if you were the same as the other cleaning companies… then competing on price may be important.

But you're NOT.

And your MGPs tell in dramatic fashion how <u>different</u> you are.

Now, with that said, we wish we could promise you every prospect will now gladly pay whatever you ask, without a fuss... but it's not quite that simple, of course!

Money isn't everything, but it does have to be dealt with; it can be an objection.

What's that?

Well, an objection is basically a "hurdle". Again, it isn't necessarily a deal breaker... *but it <u>does</u> need to be overcome.*

Why?

Well, no matter if the person you're dealing with is or is not the only decision maker, <u>they still want to make sure their decision makes sense financially!</u>

Especially if they aren't the only decision maker, they want to be prepared to defend their decision to the "higher ups"; to be able to have answers to give their boss, or their bosses' boss, about why they picked you.

Their necks are on the line too.

And they know <u>those</u> folks are going to ask about <u>the money</u>...*they always do!*

This isn't an insurmountable problem, but you'll likely have to tackle it; so, better to be prepared in advance.

Now, the way to tackle the price objection reminds us of how we once heard someone explain how a soccer player should hit, or strike, a ball with their head. (In soccer terms - a "header").

He explained… "<u>You hit</u> the soccer ball… you <u>don't</u> let the soccer ball <u>hit</u> you!"

That's PRO-active, not RE-active!

So, here we go… like hitting the soccer ball, we want to plan pro-actively how we will deal with the issue of price.

We want to "strike" it exactly as hard as we want, with the part of our head we want, exactly when we want, and in the exact direction we want. Planned, deliberate, pro-actively.

So, how exactly does striking a soccer ball "head on" apply to overcoming the price objection for janitorial cleaning programs?

Let's take a look.

First, you need to have a <u>plan</u> for clearly showing your prospects that, in addition to all the great benefits they'd enjoy from using your service… it also makes financial sense!

Basically, that it's a good VALUE.

How?

Well, by walking your prospect through your *systems, procedures and related Measurable Guarantees of Performance, showing how they <u>directly</u> translate into real dollars and cents savings* - VALUE!

- **$$** If you have a plan for keeping turnover down, you can show your prospect how much time the current cleaning company's inefficiency is "costing" them. (i.e. the cost of having to pay

85

for an excessive amount of security, administrative and training time to continually get new people authorized and approved to be in their building.)

- $$ And, while we're at it, explain to your prospects the cost of poor cleaning quality that often goes with having constantly having "new" people in the building.

Or, let's say, you have a customer service system and related MGP that guarantees "SAME DAY SERVICE".

- $$ Well, show your prospects the real dollar and cents value of only having to make <u>one</u> phone call and <u>know</u> everything will be taken care of overnight, in advance of the surprise VIP visit?

- $$ Or describe the dollar and cents value of knowing YOU actually <u>will</u> be doing the quality control, so they're no longer forced to play the role of "acting supervisor" or "cleaning police".

- $$ Or, finally, how much time and money will it save your prospect if your cleaning company handled everything regarding tracking, ordering, delivering and stocking consumable poly/ paper supplies?

How much? Plenty!

The point is this: Hopefully they're already "sold" on you.

Now, you simply need to overcome the price objection by "Showing Them The Money!"

28. Write Like You TALK

People are always asking us what their brochures, flyers or marketing letters should say.

Hopefully, by now, you have a pretty good idea.

You want to communicate your Measurable Guarantees of Performance and include other marketing tools such as:

1. Powerful Headlines

2. Testimonials

3. Measurable Guarantees of Performance, and the

4. Benefits! Benefits! Benefits... that come from your MGPs

5. Strong Calls To Action

6. Deadlines

But, here's <u>another</u> insider secret to getting people to read what you write.

Write like you talk.

Really, *write like you talk.*

What do we mean?

Well, basically it's this: You need to write like you are having a real conversation with someone. Here's why...

How much attention do <u>you</u> give a marketing brochure or flyer or letter... that simply uses the same short, cliché advertising lines we've all heard a million times before?

You know the ones.... *Licensed, Bonded and Insured! Free Estimates! - In Business Since 1985! Trained Staff! Quality Control! Frequent*

Inspections! Blah, blah, blah...

Now, don't get us wrong. We're not saying any of one of these business expressions is necessarily bad.

It's just that... they're <u>not</u> <u>good</u> <u>enough</u>!

They're tired, overused, and worn out.

And maybe worst of all...in today's super-fast-paced world of short attention spans and overloaded mail boxes filled with piles of advertising messages, it takes something <u>different</u> to cut through the clutter!

What could reach through the static and the noise to grab your prospect "by the collar" and get his or her undivided attention?

Your message told in <u>your</u> words

That's right. If you've been following along, you know how by now - how important it is that your company offers a unique and effective solution to your prospect's most pressing problems.

But, if you share that message in a "voice" that sounds the same as every one of the other thousands of competitors "voices" out there... *they may not hear your message at all!*

Using <u>your</u> "voice" means writing as if you were personally talking to someone, one on one, and you <u>knew</u> it was <u>critically</u> important they understand what you have to tell them.

If you were using <u>your</u> "voice", you wouldn't simply throw out a few standard, catch phrases like... "Free estimates" or "Satisfaction Guaranteed!"

No, to tell something that important and that real, you'd want to, *no, need to,* take the time to explain <u>why</u> you understand the trouble they're in, <u>how</u> you came up with the answer to it, and <u>exactly</u> <u>what</u> they need to do to solve their problem.

So, take your time, make it clear, make it emotional, and use <u>your</u> words. Prospects won't care about an occasional grammar mistake… if they can literally "feel you talking to them".

29. REAL Beats Clever

It's fun to think up and write something clever. You can see a lot of funny and clever things in advertising in any city in the U.S.

Our local zoo advertises from time to time on billboards around town. The billboard will have some clever or funny "play on words".

For example, let's say they're opening a panda exhibit…and the sign will say "Come down and enjoy utter p*anda-monium* at the zoo!"

Yeah, we get it. *But does it work?*

Who cares… as long as it's clever, right?

Wrong.

Don't get us wrong, we love our zoo. In fact, we've got one of the greatest zoos in the country, but to be honest...

We don't think it much matters if it works, or not.

Huh, why?

Well, our community supports our zoo big time… including financially… so… they can "afford" to be cute and clever in their advertising.

Whether the ad works well or not, the zoo will still be in business tomorrow, but…, if <u>you</u> spend a fortune on advertising that doesn't work…

You might not. *Ouch!*

Why are we being such scrooges? Don't we like things that are funny?

Sure. But, the philosophy that has gotten us where we are today is this - being REAL <u>beats</u> being clever!

What do we mean by REAL?

Well, when your marketing makes it clear that you have genuine empathy for your customer, well, that's the "stuff" that sells.

That's the "stuff" that inspires people to act.

For example, what if the zoo ran an ad that promoted the fact that they were offering a special discount to help families afford bringing the whole gang down to the zoo, and it was pitched something like this...

"We know gasoline is up this summer. But we don't want <u>that</u> to keep <u>you</u> from bringing your family to the zoo to have fun and make memories before the summer slips away; so this Saturday, we're announcing...

Take A "Bite" Out Of High Gas Prices At The Zoo!

Anyone arriving by 10 AM this Saturday can enjoy full admission for HALF OFF! That's right, half off! We realize how tough it is out there, but we're in this together. So, come down to the Zoo and make memories your family will treasure for a lifetime!

Now, how do YOU think that compares to "Come on down to the zoo, don't miss the panda-monium" as far as reaching out and getting you to respond by giving you what you want!

By the way, you can still be clever, but the point is - don't <u>only</u> be clever. Start with something <u>more</u> - real empathy!

30. Use Hi-Octane HEADLINES

For your sales letters to generate lots of interest from prospects try using "Hi-Octane" headlines.

What are "Hi-Octane" headlines?

Well, let's first say what they're not.

Hi-Octane headlines are not lies, half truths or outlandish promises meant only to shock the reader.

For example, here's what we're NOT talking about: 'Call "We're Perfect!" Cleaning…where we promise to do every thing perfectly every night, guaranteed, or you'll get triple your money back!'

Simply promising the moon in your headline to get the attention of your prospect doesn't work. Your prospects know better, and so do you. So…

What <u>does</u> work?

Well, let's look at a famous headline that provides a good example of a Hi-Octane Headline:

Do you remember Domino Pizza's guarantee from years ago- "Fresh, Hot Pizza… delivered in 30 minutes or less, or it's FREE!"

This headline, this guarantee, was incredibly successful for Domino's and helps to show what <u>does</u> work in headlines for ads, especially for ads in the service industry.

And that, as we've discussed, is highlighting powerful MGPs, or, Measurable Guarantees of Performance.

So, what might an effective Hi-Octane Headline for an office cleaning business look like? Well, how about...

"What If Only ONE Local Cleaning Company <u>Guaranteed</u> You'd Be 100% Thrilled With <u>Every</u> Cleaning or it's FREE?"

<u>*Our Quality Guarantee*</u>:

"You'll Be 100% Delighted With The Quality and Level of Service Of Each Cleaning Visit… or it's FREE!" *

* To guarantee you get the quality of cleaning you deserve, your building will be thoroughly inspected each night using our special nightly "QC Check", which will be "graded", faxed to our office and placed on your desk. If you ever disagree with a daily "grade", or are not 100% satisfied with a cleaning…it's FREE!

31. People LOVE Free!

You probably already realize people like getting something for FREE. So, why are we devoting an entire section of the book to this idea? Well, because

…they just don't "like" FREE, they LOVE IT!

That's right, and it's not just a general feeling, or hunch, that people like FREE. Nope, studies confirm it.

In fact, we recall reading about one study reporting nearly 75% of consumers felt getting a FREE offer, basically "something for nothing", got them interested in trying a new or different product or service… *more than anything else!*

And, here's another thing, it's not just a group here or a group there that's motivated by FREE, it's nearly everyone… *across the board.*

You see, this marketing principle is about as <u>universal</u> as you'll ever find.

That's right, from 'average Joe' who grabs the "buy one - get one free" deal at the movie rental store, to 'fat cat Fred' who test drives a sports car because he's been told if he does, he'll get a FREE set of golf club covers - nobody is immune to the power of FREE!

So, what should you offer for FREE?

Well, it sure isn't just a FREE estimate. Seriously, is there anyone out there today who would even consider actually paying for an estimate on cleaning their building?

Well, if offering a free estimate is about as tired and worn out as they come... what else is there to offer?

Plenty.

How about, for example, a <u>FREE REPORT</u> about something very important to your customer.

Or how about a series of special reports you offer in your marketing pieces on topics such as:

Get Your FREE Special Report:

"Green" Cleaning - What You Need To Know Now! or "NEW Cleaning Equipment Guaranteed To Improve Your Building's Appearance And Save You Money!"

You get the idea. Or here's another FREEBIE idea that's sure to please...

During February ONLY, You'll Get A **FREE Building Measurement Report** When You Call To Have Us Prepare A Cleaning Proposal, For Your Building, Giving You An Amazing Breakdown Of Your Facilities... that's right, FREE!

Your customer gets a FREE report. You get a chance to "talk" one-on-

one with a customer whose asking to learn more about you.

FREE to them - priceless to you.

32. P.S. The Most Important Thing… LAST

Some things in life defy logic.

The ant shouldn't be able to lift 10 or 20 or even 50 times its weight, but they do. It doesn't seem logical, but then some things in life and in business just aren't logical.

In marketing, the importance of a P.S. is like that.

That's right, a P.S. or Postscript at the end of a marketing letter is very important…even though most people wouldn't think so.

Most people think of a P.S. as just an afterthought; just something you quickly add to the end of a letter.

They couldn't be more wrong.

In fact, many people check out and pay more attention to what you say in your P.S. than to nearly anything else in your marketing piece.

So, here's the tip…. make it count.

That's right! So, whatever you put in your P.S. make it powerful and make it work for you.

What could it be? Well, here are three ideas:

P.S. Remember, you NEED to call by 4:30 PM Friday, August 12th to get a FREE exterior window cleaning for your building when we submit a cleaning proposal for your consideration!!!

or

P.S.S. Hurry! Schedule your carpet cleaning job by July 31 to get your FREE 4 ft. walk-off mat to protect your freshly cleaned carpets!

or

P.S.S.S. Don't forget... when you sign up by 12:00 PM, Thursday April 8, to start having us track, order and stock your consumable poly/paper products, we'll give you a full case of toilet tissue absolutely FREE with your first order!

33. A Photo's Worth A Thousand Words

We've all heard it a million times, "A picture is worth a thousand words."

Well, so is a PHOTO.

Why?

Well, because people like to buy from people - real *flesh and bones* people.

They just do. And if you think about it, you'll probably agree that you do too. It's natural.

So, that's the important marketing purpose including a photo of yourself in ads provides...

It connects a human face to your company.

And when you put your name underneath your photo, which you should always do, you've then, of course, given them *"a name to put with the face"*.

So, why do prospective buyers respond to seeing a photo of, in this case, the owner of the business?

Well, there is probably a whole list of reasons, but the obvious ones are, well.... obvious.

- It creates interest and it provides a connection.

- It personalizes the often impersonal process of finding a cleaning company

But a PHOTO is different. It's real. There's no where to hide.

Plus, we tend to trust pictures.

Most of us share a belief that, as the saying goes, "Pictures don't lie". For example, you've probably heard people saying let's "go to the video tape" when they want to prove something one way or the other.

Subconsciously, we believe, if we can just see the salesman's face, their eyes - something, we can know if they'll be truthful with us. We'll have made a personal connection.

It points to our strong desire to know who we're doing business with. And one way you can give your customer a very real look at who they're doing business with, is to paste your lovely "mug" right there on the marketing piece.

34. What's In A NAME?

What does your company name say about you?

Think about yours. Say it a few times. Write it down; look at it for a minute. What does it say to you?

Does it send the message you want it to? Does it say you are credible, experienced, professional?

People often ask if they should change the name of their company to something different, maybe more professional.

Well, of course, that depends on you, your personality and what you want your corporate image to be?

Do you want it to be folksy? friendly? Do you want it to be credible? confident?

Many companies change their names over time.

We changed ours several times.

We started off with the name Jim's Cleaning; no surprise there, Jim was the name of the previous owner.

But, later we changed the name to Toledo Commercial Cleaning Inc. It worked well for years, until we grew to service cities well beyond Toledo.

And, then, finally we changed our name to Clean Care Inc..

This name suited us well; allowing us to market ourselves outside Toledo and giving us the flexibility to market all kinds of cleaning services.

So, the short answer is – yes! While by no means the only, or even biggest, key to business success, name changes can be helpful in positioning your company in the marketplace.

It does involve some expense (legal to check name availability, office expense to change letterhead, invoices etc.) aggravation (legal name change/ tax forms etc.) and confusion (explanation to your customers). So, it's not as simple as 'wiggling your nose'.

BUT, if it can move your company image forward and help you GROW, it can be time and money well spent!

35. It's All about Having a GREAT Website, Right?

No doubt about it, your prospects, like you, turn to the computer many times every day. And that also holds true when they're trying to find a new cleaning company.

Sure, they may pull out their "CLEANING" file from their cabinet filled with information from local janitorial companies, but they also increasingly just go online.

So, what should you do <u>online</u>?
Well, first, and foremost, is to develop a web site that's more than just a billboard about you.

Like all of your marketing, it needs to do <u>more</u> than report your *name, rank and serial number*. Instead, you need it to be a professional and complete salesperson for you every day all day.

To do that, <u>you need to include the elements that make any marketing effective</u>, whether it's online or off-line, such as:

- Grabbing attention with powerful headlines, sub-heads highlighting Measurable Guarantees of Performance etc.

- Earning trust - by sharing your story (i.e. bio, photos) and the first hand reports of others using your services (testimonials)

- Driving the important benefit messages that dramatize the stark difference between you and your competition. (i.e. MGP)

- Asking for the sale with a clear call to action and strong offer (i.e. compelling)

- Making it easy to do business with you now; or if not quite ready, even easier to learn more about you (i.e. free report)

- Building a bigger (number), but also better (qualified) list of prospects interested in what you have to say, and <u>willing to give you permission</u> to share it with them. (i.e. opt-in)

36. Our BIGGEST Mistake

For goodness sakes, don't make the BIG mistake we made.

And, here it is... drum roll... **to stop marketing!**

Now, we'll admit when you first hear it, it's easy to think, "Don't worry, we'll never do that!" Really?

Let us tell you a quick story...

There was a time, years ago, when things were going pretty well for our cleaning business. We felt we had enough accounts, and we were finally making a nice little profit to boot.

In short, we felt pretty satisfied. That's right; we sat back and enjoyed a much-needed sigh of relief. Ahhhhh...

We told ourselves it was OK to slow down, and stop our marketing efforts for a little while. Why not? We were already "busy" and it would give us time to get "caught up" on "loose ends". Uh huh, you guessed it. Big mistake!

Suddenly, we lost 3 accounts!

It happened in just a couple of weeks, but sure felt like it happened all at once. One customer was going to re-locate, another account, which was really important to us was going to have a couple of their own employees take care of the cleaning, and we can't remember what the deal was at the 3rd place.

Anyway…Ouch! Losing one of our accounts would have hurt... but all three <u>really</u> stung!

So we scrambled!

That's right! We we're so shook up, we immediately went cold calling like crazy, up and down the major industrial developments, racing to get more business to replace the ones we lost.

It was scary and we hated it. That part we remember clearly. And we vowed to never let it happen again.

The good news, it doesn't have to happen to you ... if you make a commitment to <u>never</u> stop marketing and selling.

Remember: <u>On-going marketing is the KEY!</u>

PART II
HOW TO LAND

INSIDER SECRET #4
Aim to Be NEXT:
The Secret to Selling Cleaning

37. Aim To Be NEXT: What Is It?

Well, if you want to grow like crazy in the cleaning biz, here's a secret:

Aim to be <u>NEXT</u>! Not second, but NEXT!

Next in line.

Next, in the mind of your prospect.

If your prospect is looking at switching cleaning services for whatever reasons, you want to be the NEXT cleaning company they'd *give a shot* at their building.

Cleaning is a "funny" business.

It's a daily challenge for the owner of any cleaning business to make sure everything goes smooth - in every building - every night.

Don't miss a trash. Don't forget to lock a door. And of course, hope they like, or at least get along with, the latest cleaning person you put on the account.

It's a lot that has to go right.

You try hard to make everything go smoothly so the customer doesn't get upset and decide to take his business elsewhere.

In a business, like cleaning, where so much can wrong, if a company isn't "on their toes" at all times, it can often be just a matter of time before problems boil over...and suddenly, the building manager moves quickly to make a change.

So what can you do?

Find a way to take advantage of the often fragile, sometimes unpredictable nature of cleaning, by how you position your company.

You want to position your company as THE cleaning company the prospect would consider the NEXT time they look to make any change.

You want to be "waiting in the wings"; You want to be <u>next in line</u>.

Like the baseball coach that walks to the mound, and touches his left or right arm to make a pitching change...you want your prospect to pick up his phone and automatically call YOU!

In other words, rather than frantically chasing your prospects, the "Aim To Be Next" strategy consistently ATTRACTS them to you!

Fine, But How?

Well, truthfully, it's many things. But here are a couple important ones:

First, rather than use high-pressure telemarketing, where someone ends up having to "talk a prospect" into letting you stop out to bid, you know we prefer you send a <u>series of powerful messages</u> that **consistently**

highlights how you, unlike your competitors, can consistently get them what they want.

Why is it so important the messages be ongoing?

Well, because you never know when something will happen to "upset the apple cart" and a prospect will be looking to make a change.

That's one way you can successfully "Aim To Be Next". Here's another...

Second, they need to know you're genuinely on their side.

They need to know you're honestly looking out for them, and what's best for them. Now, if that happens to be hiring you now, great.

But, if NOW is not the time... that's perfectly fine too.

So, we're not in the business of "strong arming" people to hire us. Instead, over time, we want to have them naturally, almost *automatically*, come to see us as the next logical answer, and best choice for them in cleaning contractors.

Not Necessarily Now, but NEXT.

Let's look at this a little closer.

Many cleaning contractors approach the sale process like it's a war; a war which must be won at all costs - and won today! They see their job as convincing the prospect they:

1. . ...must make a change,

2. . ...must choose only their cleaning company, and

3. . ...must do it now!

Now, compare that approach with our strategy of "aiming to be next", or consulting, with a prospect to position your company as the NEXT credible solution to their problem.

The Feeling Is Completely Different.

When "aiming to be next", we **naturally** introduce ourselves to our prospect, **deliberately** but without pressure uncover problems they are facing, and **genuinely** offer ideas and suggestions.

We want them to know we are on their side, because we really are. Whether we get the account today, or the next time around, we are on their side.

But for this philosophy to work - **you've got to mean it!**

If dogs can "smell fear" then prospects can "smell insincerity". People know if you're sincerely looking out for their best interest, or just looking to "make the sale".

Here are a few common mistakes to avoid:

- Quickly agreeing to nearly anything, no matter what

- Saying only what you think the prospect "wants to hear"

- Answering without thinking

- Agreeing without checking

- Speaking too fast and rushing through things

And boy, can prospects sense "trouble" when a salesperson is told they did not get the account and then reacts negatively in any of the following ways:

- Seems irritated or angry

- Cuts the conversation short

- Rushes off in a huff

- Never calls back again

If you were "aiming to be next", and really looking out for the prospect, you would <u>never</u> do any of these things.

You would be supportive of whatever choice they've made, and use it as a way of "locking yourself in" with them by the way you handle rejection.

What Do I Mean?

Well, when you "Aim to Be Next", you <u>take the pressure out of the selling process.</u>

If the prospective client wants to hire you right now, great! But it's also fine if they hire you during the next go 'round as well.

Hint... *the funny thing is...* when it's not so critically important that you're hired right away, it makes everyone feel less pressure, and the whole sales process runs more smoothly.

You may even stand a BETTER chance of getting the job NOW!

We can't tell you how many times we weren't given the account the first time around. But, we made a point of supporting the prospective client and their decision; while always letting them know we were ready to help whenever they needed us.

Time and time again, we would eventually get those accounts.

Often, in a very short time!

And, we believe it was because of the strong and helpful, but *not desperate*, approach we maintained throughout the process.

What powerful message do you think it sends to a prospect when you continue to be interested, supportive and helpful to them… even after you didn't get the account this time around?

You Don't Have To Win Every Battle… To Win The War

You might be thinking… that sounds great, but

"How can I be "easy going" and act as a "consultant" when I desperately need more business and feel the intense pressure of landing an account?"

Great question. Here's the answer…**Never stop marketing.**

When you have a steady enough flow of new leads coming in, you won't feel such intense pressure to land any given one of them because you know there's plenty more lined up right behind them.

38. MEASURE for Marketing Power

Getting a calculated cleaning time for office cleaning jobs you're bidding on, by gathering the actual dimensions, or at the very least the cleanable sq. ft. by area, is important.

How else will you be able to determine a price that's competitive, while allowing for the necessary time to clean?

That alone is reason enough for going through a building to write down the measurements. But, the good news is… you get even more "bang for your buck" for the time you spend measuring.

That's right, there's even more value… and it's BIG. To explain, let us tell you something that happened to us.

We were doing a walk-through of a building and the prospect had just finished giving us the "tour". We started to jot down some of the measurements, when our "tour guide" asked what we were writing down.

We explained we were gathering information about their building including measurements by type of area, (office, conference room etc.) along with noting the floor types and number of fixtures (toilets, sinks etc.) in order to *workload* their building.

We went on to explain we have found it to be the best way to properly determine how long it should take to deliver professional office cleaning services for their building at a fair and competitive price.

Here's the important thing: Our prospect was very impressed, commenting that no other cleaning company she'd ever given a "tour" of the building to before, *had ever measured or counted anything!*

In fact, she said "They just kind of walked along, nodding to everything she said, and then left the building with just a few notes and no measurements at all."

You stand out from the crowd when you take the time to record measurements and related building information during your walk through.

In an industry too often saddled with the negative stereotype of being unprofessional, measuring a building is a GOLDEN opportunity to break out of the mold!

Show you're a "cut above" by accurately measuring the building you're bidding on. It highlights your attention to detail.

You won't have to convince them you know what you're doing, ...it will be obvious you're not simply "throwing darts at a board", when they see you are actually calculating a professional, budgeted cleaning time.

You can expect your prospects to project this positive opinion of you and your bidding style into an overall positive opinion of your cleaning company as well. And that's a good thing!

39. Bid Cover Letters with MUSCLE

Frankly, most people think of a bid cover letter as a *weak*, nearly meaningless, part of any proposal - nothing more than a formality.

Don't believe it!

It couldn't be further from the truth! In fact, put it together the RIGHT way, and your bid cover letter can become one of the most powerful sales tools in your proposal.

Most cleaning companies put very little thought, and even less effort, into the cover letter. To them, it's just a short, meaningless page they feel *forced* to include, if for no other reason than they think it makes them look "professional".

Most cover letters simply spit out the same safe, but boring "stuff" that has "put prospects to sleep" for years. - "Thanks for allowing us to bid"… "We appreciate your interest"… blah, blah, blah."

But, *if it bores you*, you can pretty safely assume…

It's boring your prospects too!

It's not the cover letter that's the problem; it's what it says about us, as the cleaning contractor, that's the real problem!

And what's that?

Well, it shows we didn't think it was necessary to take the time to highlight those important details, duties, issues and areas the customer told us about their building.

You need to see the cover letter as a powerful tool to forcefully attract your prospect to WANT to do business with you, and you alone!

The bid cover letter gives you that opportunity. Don't miss it.

First, don't get us wrong; it's ok to use some of the standard language you're used to seeing in professional bid cover letters such as "Thanks for taking the time to show us your facility" or "As you review the bid, feel free to call us with any questions."

But that's just the beginning.

That's right! Use the cover letter as the place to:

1. Clearly show that you have heard your prospects complaints, concerns and issues LOUD AND CLEAR

2. Understand them, care about them and

3. Have a definite plan for solving them and keeping them solved.

When your prospect reads through a bid cover letter with MUSCLE; one that lists not only their main concerns and problems, but describes in detail the actual systems and procedures you will use to correct them... they'll be impressed, not bored!

So, remember to take time to "go over" the points covered in your cover letter. You put real work into writing it...make sure your prospect sees it and understands it, so they can hopefully appreciate it for what it represents.

40. Who Needs REFERENCES?

Short and sweet? *You do!*

And what exactly is a reference?

Well, it's a customer that is so satisfied with you and your cleaning, they're willing to inconvenience themselves... *for you!*

What do we mean? Well, let's think about it.

Customers of yours, who agree to be listed as a reference of yours, are saying they're willing to "take calls" during their busy work day to answer questions about you and your cleaning company.

Now, that's commitment. That's loyalty.

Written, audio and video testimonials are great... and you need to collect and exhibit them prominently as "<u>proof</u>" of your company's ability to <u>deliver</u> on your promises of service; but, "live" references are just as necessary.

They say to the prospect, "this cleaning company has a number of clients so happy with their service, they're willing... even glad, to tell others about it!

Don't panic. You don't need <u>50</u>.

But you do want to assemble <u>several</u> as quickly as possible - so all the reference calls don't come *crashing down* onto just <u>one</u> unsuspecting "guy" or "gal", who kindly agreed to act as a reference, not knowing... *they were the only one!*

One is better than none... but you <u>do</u> want to get, oh, let's say at least three or four, as soon as you can, and eventually, have six, seven or eight of them if possible.

When you begin to have that many, you begin to send the full message of confidence in your company that you want to send.

Some companies have so many, they're able to customize the list they include with their proposal to match the kind of building they're bidding on. (i.e. bank references if they're bidding on banks, etc.)

That's great, but you only need one to start. From there, you'll need to be proactive; don't kid yourself, customers don't generally call you "out of the blue" and ask,

"Hey, we were just thinking about you. You clean our offices so well, that we were thinking you might need a reference, and wondered if you might like to use us?"

We suppose it's happened; but not very often.

And it <u>doesn't</u> make your customers *inconsiderate* for not offering without being asked; not at all.

It's like a lot of things - If it is to be...it's up to me! (or you, in this case) That's right.

<u>You</u> need to step up and ask.

Just like getting testimonials; people aren't *mind readers*. But if you do step up and ask, you'll find many of them more than willing to help you out... as long as you've been delivering a professional level of service to them.

And when they do agree to be on your list of references, you'll have a real asset.

41. NEVER Hear "Your Price Is Too High!" Again

How'd you like to never hear, "Your Price is Too High" ever again?

Sounds too good to be true, we know, but hear us out for a minute, and see if you don't agree it might just be possible - if you know how!

Nothing is more frustrating than to put a lot of work into preparing a professional cleaning proposal, only to hear a week later,

"Sorry, your price was too high; we went with someone else!"

Well, here is a strategy that might just keep that from happening to you ever again. Here's how it works:

Take more time up front with the prospective client. Sit down with them. Learn what they want. Find out what they don't need done.

And when you get the measurements of the building, take the time to mark down which areas are difficult, and which look easy to clean.

Talk with your client. Slow things down. Then, go back to your office and run the numbers.

Now, here's the strategy:

Meet with them a 2nd time. You can explain you need to get one more measurement, or double-check a couple measurements in a certain part of the building; *whatever.*

And also mention you need a little time to go over a few last questions that came up as you were working on their bid.

That's it. No big deal.

When you meet, sit down and slowly show them your information: measurements, summaries, specs, time estimates AND then here's the important part.

Explain how you understand budgets are important today more than ever, so you'd like to go ahead and explain how things look now, as far as price, to see if it's in the budget "ballpark".

You can go on to explain that these are just "preliminary figures"; nothing necessarily "carved in stone"; simply based on initial settings for cleaning tasks and frequencies you've laid out.

Then, you can mention how you can nearly always work on the details of the duties and frequencies with a client to come up with a program that meets both their service as well as budget requirements.

Finally, you can tell them where the initial price is coming in at, or, at least the price range.

Here's the thing:

You want to see if the cleaning program, budgeted hours and monthly price you're preparing for them not only gives them the cleaning they want, but also, at a price they're willing to consider.

Frankly, it's no fun to find out you've prepared a program with a monthly price they are flat out NOT willing to pay. So, it can be helpful to find out now, when you still have a chance and the time to work out an alternative plan.

The alternative program can be a closer match of duties and price - that satisfies both you and the prospect.

Important Note: This isn't a *chess game* about price. As we've explained earlier, you need to make your prospective client keenly aware of the real *financial* (as well as building appearance) value of your unique systems and procedures - the ones that allow you to back your service with compelling MGPs.

In summary, you need to clearly explain price in the context of EVERYTHING you bring to them - that makes that your price a great VALUE.

But let's get back to where we left off.

Now, once you tell them what the monthly price is coming in at, you can simply ask them, " How does that fit with what you were expecting… budget-wise?"

Then be quiet.

You need to patiently wait for an answer.

In many cases, we have found prospective clients surprisingly willing to discuss the price issue, if we're willing to listen.

Either way, isn't it better to deal with any price objection NOW before they look at 3 or 4 other quotes, and simply award it to someone else... without you having a chance to respond?

The worst that can happen is they say, "We're sorry, we can't, or won't tell you, what we're paying."

No problem. No need to get defensive.

If this happens, you just calmly explain that that's fine, and you will proceed with the plan, using the duties they gave you, or the standard layout you normally recommend for this kind of project.

But, if instead your prospective client volunteers that your price is "in the ball park"; well, then, "You're gold!

Now, you know can proceed with confidence.

On the other hand, if they say, "Well, honestly, you're high; we wasn't thinking of paying that much"

Well, fine. At least, you can work on a solution together. There's lots of ways to go about fixing the problem:

- Changes to duties,

- Changes to frequencies,

- Eliminating or cutting-back cleaning in certain areas

- Optional programs such as light/heavy schedules

At best, you're well on your way to closing the sale, and at worst, you've learned more clearly what the customer is actually looking for from a cleaning service in the areas of price and service.

42. STEPS to a Winning Walkthrough

The first key to a winning walkthrough, which is basically your on-site visit to meet the prospect and measure their building, may not be what you expect.

It's your **MIND SET**.

That's right, it's the attitude you keep before, during and after the walk-through.

We know. We know. We hate to start with something as hard to think about as "mindset"- but we've got to do it, because… it's the *thing* that affects everything else!

So, what should your mind set be?

Well, you should keep a calm, open, professional, "interested" attitude. Does this remind you of our "Aim To Be Next" philosophy discussed before? It should.

We want to have the mind set of a problem-solver. And finally, we want to maintain a mind set of attracting business to us... rather than chasing after it.

So let's see what this kind of mind set would look like, even before the actual walk through begins.

Next, we want to arrive to the building in advance, so we can be sure to walk in to the appointment at the "right time".

And what time is that?

You want to walk into the lobby for your appointment **5 minutes early**, <u>not</u> 15 minutes early; and certainly <u>not</u> late. Why?

Well, 5 minutes early is interested and professional. 15 minutes early is too <u>needy</u>. And late, of course, is <u>unacceptable</u>!

And finally, you want to arrive dressed properly in business attire. You need to use your judgment here.

Some cleaning contractors would never consider arriving for a walk through in anything less than a business suit and tie. However, others, including myself, find that a clean business shirt with your logo etc. is just fine too - as long as you're looking professional.

Remember the old saying, <u>"Look Sharp- Be Sharp!"</u>

Next, let's look at how the first person you meet when you arrive to do a walk through - the receptionist, is so important.

43. Your Friend the RECEPTIONIST

In most cases, the first person you meet is the receptionist.

And, how you treat the receptionist tells a lot about you, sets the tone of the walk-through, and sometimes may actually determine whether you ultimately get the job!

Don't believe us?

Ok. Think about this for a minute.

What means more to the prospect, "What you say about yourself" or "What others say about you"?

That's right, we've talked about this before, when we were discussing the value of testimonials. And generally, the answer is, "What others say about you" because first hand reports about you are more believable.

So, let's get back to the receptionist.

Have you ever noticed when your contact walks you out to the lobby, when your appointment is done… and you're about to leave, WHO is there next to the contact as you walk out the door?

That's right - the receptionist!

Yes, the receptionist. That same receptionist you spoke with just 30 minutes or an hour ago.

And if you <u>don't</u> think the receptionist and the contact very often take a second to chat about you after you're out the door… *then you're crazier than half the politicians in Washington!*

The truth, of course, is they often <u>do</u> talk about you when you walk to your car and what the receptionist says about you can make a difference in how things are going to "go" for you.

Sometimes, it's just a small thing, like:

Receptionist: "He seemed very nice and professional"

Contact: "Yes, I thought so too!"

If you impressed him or her with your respect and professional manner, you may have just got some FREE, but <u>priceless</u> PR delivered to your contact.

On the other hand, if the conversation goes more like:

Receptionist "Boy, I've got to tell you Sue, he was so rude and pushy when he first came in. I was surprised."

Contact: "Really, thanks for telling me that. Hmmm ... we'll see."

Not good.

So, follow the advice we hopefully all got at a very young age, "Treat everybody the way you'd like to be treated."

Mom, of course, was right... again!

44. Are You Too NEEDY?

No disrespect. It's really more of a <u>business</u> question, than a personal one.

Put another way, what message are you projecting to your prospects?

Think about it a minute. Does the way you do business send the message that you're a <u>busy</u> and <u>successful</u> professional?

Well, if you're like many well-intentioned cleaning contractors, you may be sending a quite different message than the one you want to send.

It's an easy trap to fall into.

Why?

Well, because among other reasons, from a very early age we are taught to be helpful, generous, and available to others in need. And those are all good qualities!

But, and this is a big but, you have to be careful that in an effort to be helpful, available and generous, you don't position yourself as too helpful, too available, and too generous!

What do we mean? *Let's take a closer look...*

What if, for example, you called your doctor, and after the phone rang just once… they *personally* answered the phone. Yeah, we're talking about your doctor actually taking the incoming call and helping to schedule your appointment!!

What would you think of that?

Try to avoid answering too quickly with a knee jerk response of, "Great, I'm glad they can take my call personally."

Really? Is that *really* what you would think?

Or might you instead actually wonder, "What's going on here? If my physician is a busy, highly skilled and trained professional, how in the world could he or she possibly be personally answering the phone?"

What message might this kind of unlimited availability <u>actually</u> be sending?

Let's look at another example. Let's say an attorney. What if you needed expert legal advice, called a prominent and well respected lawyer's office, and the attorney actually answered the phone greeting you with "Hi, this is Joe, the attorney, what can I do for you today?"

Now, it might be that in both cases, the doctor and the attorney are actually excellent, highly qualified professionals.

But the point is; what marketing message does it send to current and prospective clients, when your professional expert appears to be too available?

It can be *unsettling.*

Let's be clear. We're not suggesting you provide less than quality follow up to prospects, or less than good customer service to current clients.

But what we are suggesting is to consider changes to your selling approach, marketing systems and customer service practices to project a professional, but not too needy image that <u>attracts</u> rather than repels business.

Ever noticed when you frantically pursue something, the less likely you may be to get it, and the more likely you are to actually drive it further away.

How about this for example:

Let's say you finally get the opportunity to submit a proposal for a building you've always wanted to clean.

And, in a genuine, *but misguided* effort, to be helpful, you anxiously call them back every day or so, just to "check in" to see if they've made a decision - only to find the <u>more</u> you called the <u>less</u> interested they become... until they turn "cold" to you altogether.

You may be left throwing your hands up in frustration, saying "Why won't they just make up their minds?!"

Maybe this has happened to you.

It's certainly happened to us. It's not just <u>what</u> we say....it's <u>how</u>, and <u>when</u> we choose to say it.

When we're too needy, when we <u>really</u> want the job, if we're not careful, we can find ourselves going too far; we may call too much, and end up "repelling rather than attracting" business.

And, on a related topic...

45. Don't AUTOMATICALLY Agree

When selling, you want to be a "Welcome!" mat... *not a door mat!*

It's true; shooting straight with a prospect about what <u>is</u>, and sometimes, more importantly, what <u>isn't</u> possible, is simply a better approach than *mindlessly* agreeing to any request thrown at you during the selling process.

Now, we expect some may feel that following this advice, of correcting, disagreeing with, or even saying NO to a prospective customer is *reckless* at best, and in some cases, a virtual recipe for a sales disaster!

We understand.

We felt that same way ourselves, years ago, at a time when we were so anxious, nervous, and yes, desperate to land new accounts we probably would have said yes to nearly anything - no matter how ridiculous.

But, that was then, and <u>this</u> is NOW!

And <u>now</u>, we know better! And hopefully, you'll know better too - a lot earlier in the game than we did.

You see, now we know, if we provide a quality cleaning service to our customers, then not only are we allowed to have limits to what we offer, but <u>prospects expect us to have limits,</u> as long as ...those limits are reasonable.

Be sure to explain <u>why</u> limits are important!

In fact, when you explain the reasons behind your decisions, you can actually <u>increase</u> your credibility with your prospect.

Doesn't that make sense? Take this example,

If you're interviewing applicants for a job and the applicant quickly snaps back with a fast "No problem!" to every-single-one of your questions, no matter what the question is... don't you actually begin to have your doubts?

Really, how can absolutely <u>everything</u> be "No problem!"

Wouldn't you, in fact, select the applicant who answers your questions honestly and <u>thoughtfully</u>, even though they may not necessarily agree with everything you say, or agree to everything you ask for.

In this way, don't they <u>actually</u> begin to earn your respect? We think so too.

Why?

You want the "real deal". Your prospects do too!

And the real deal is someone who is accommodating, while still having the confidence in themselves to occasionally say "no" to some requests when necessary.

Prospects are always "sizing you up", "checking you out" to see if you're the <u>real</u> deal.

46. Don't TRASH the Competition

We've all been tempted.

You're walking down hallways, and in and out of offices and restrooms, being shown a building to bid on...and suddenly there it is... staring you in the face... the perfect opportunity!

What is it?

Well, it could be a white painted door heading to the plant covered in greasy handprints, or it might be the tops of office partitions covered with what you consider an "inch" of dust. Or maybe it's the toilet stools in the bathroom stained with ugly mop and splash marks up the side.

Whatever it is, you're tempted to jump in and "pounce" on this chance to criticize the current service.

But don't.

We know you could...and we know you <u>want</u> to...but, again, just don't! It's not worth it.

See, if you do, you're really missing the **bigger** opportunity here.

That's right, any company... maybe every company they've brought through before, *ranted* about how bad the place looked. And those same janitorial cleaning companies also probably jumped at the chance to say...

"Yes, we can see why you're looking to fire your current cleaning company! They're really bad; this place looks just awful".

"You may even want to finish with, "We're much better than this. We would never let this kind of thing happen."

We strongly suggest you DON'T. **Ever.**

There's a much better way to highlight your company, and it <u>doesn't</u> involve...*making "mince meat" out of the other guy.*

Instead, let's say while doing a walkthrough you see a number of very obvious examples of poor cleaning, and your prospect goes so far as to say, "Well, you can see for yourself why we're going to get rid of them!

Stop.

Rather than feeling justified to pounce in with, "I sure can; they're really missing a lot!" consider instead, simply acknowledging that you do see what they are pointing out.

Then, rather than "piling on", go on to say something like this...

"Well, you know, Steve, we've found as long as we do a good job of screening and hiring, most folks can do a very good job if they're given the right training and direction. It keeps the cleaner interested and on track."

"We certainly don't have any *magic words* to make cleaning easy. It's hard work, plain and simple."

"But what we <u>do</u> have is a set of useful systems we stick with all the time. And that handful of systems forces us to handle things like training, inspections, quality control and supervision in a certain way... all the time."

"I'll go over in more detail how those systems work when I come back in with your proposal next week."

Or, instead, you may, if time permits, go on to explain,

"Here's an example. In a building like this, we would have a site-supervisor who would be responsible for certain things getting done ...every visit.

For example, they would meet with the whole cleaning staff for a few minutes at the start of each shift to spell out what extra details need to be done in which areas of the building that night.

They would also be the one to complete a short, but required, daily checklist from doing a walkthrough of the building.

It only takes about 15 minutes, but it's one way we make sure important things get done each night.

And then that form is initialed and faxed to our office each evening.

And you get a copy if you'd like. We've had just great results with that system!"

WOW, different isn't it?

Now let us ask you this....

Which approach would have the prospect <u>wanting</u> to hire you because they now see <u>you</u> as a professional with real answers to their real problems?

Would it be the approach where you "slam" the current service for being incompetent and lazy, or....

Would it be the second approach, where you clearly describe how you have <u>systems</u> to get them what they want?

We think so too!

47. Clean-Up Your NOTES

Let us tell you a story....

Years ago, we had just finished "plowing" through a long and difficult bid walk through of a building.

It was a handful.

Our contact was in a hurry, so for nearly an hour and a half, we were practically "running" through the different break rooms, restrooms, and locker rooms scattered throughout several buildings.

In the plant, we climbed up and down staircases, and in and out of hallways, to get to all the areas needing to be measured.

And as we ran from one area to the next, we frantically jotted down all the measurements, item counts and floor surfaces as fast as we could.

By the time we got done, we were *whipped.*

We walked out to our car, threw our notes on the back seat and immediately drove off. We were tired and didn't get back to work on the bid for a couple days.

And that's where the problems started.

That's right, by the time we got back to look at our notes, we had a hard time remembering a lot of the specifics.

Our notes weren't much help.

We could barely read some of them. We'd scribbled them down so quickly as we ran through the building, that only a couple days later, *the short hand scribbles were hardly recognizable.*

But, it didn't have to be that way.

Sure, we could have made our notes clearer as we ran through the bid walk-through; but to be honest, we were doing the best we could to jot something down without "holding up" our prospect any longer than necessary.

What could we have done instead?

We could have taken just another 10 minutes or so to clean up our notes in the car before leaving the parking lot... *while everything was still fresh in our minds!*

We know it sounds like a small thing. And maybe it is; but..

It works.

That's right, little strategies like taking a few minutes after every bid to get all your notes "cleaned up" can make bidding a lot easier when you get back to the office.

Don't make the costly mistake we used to make... out of pure laziness. Instead, *work smart, not hard.*

Learning and IMPLEMENTING a series of "little" improvements can move you quickly from good... to great!

48. Prospects Leave CLUES!

Prospects leave valuable "clues" for us.

And if we learn to look for, listen for and react to these "clues" in the right way, we can dramatically improve our chances of success during the walk through, or really during any visit, with our prospect.

So, let's get to it, what are these clues? What do they look like?

Well, let's look at a few examples.

If your prospect comes to the lobby to get you, but, rather than take you back to their office to talk, they quickly blurt out that they "have a lot going on", but you can "feel free to walk around to look around on your own... if you want."

It's a clue.

If you notice they're talking short and fast, seem distracted and stressed out, and seemed to be rushing you, constantly checking their watch - that's a clue too.

Now, if on the other hand, they take their time to walk you back to their office, seem more than willing to "visit" a little, and are in no particular hurry...

You get the idea, - that's a clue as well.

We're sure you get the point by now. And it probably seems so obvious it may hardly even need to be said, but let's spell it out anyway. Whatever the clue is...

Don't ignore it, pretending it doesn't matter....*It does!*

In the same way, if your prospect wants to get to know you a little bit, and seems to want to "visit" a while at first - well, to snub your nose at them, and plow right on to business issues can be a recipe for disaster too.

Instead, when you spot these "clues" of how a prospect wants to proceed - deal with them the right way.

For example, if the clues indicate the prospect is pressured on the morning you arrive, you might explain,

"Hey, Steve, I can see you've got a lot going on this morning", and then go on to suggest a way to make things a little easier, such as:

"So, if you only have the time to give me a "quick tour", that's fine, just show me what you think I need to see now, and I'll "take care of things from there" on my own, then I'll call back to arrange to get together to go over things."

or

"So, let me get out of your hair for now, and we'll just set this up when it's better for you. How would that be?"

Now, on the other hand, if you realize your prospect is taking a minute to "sit back" in their chair, trying to make small talk with you, then, *for heaven's sake*, "visit" a while.

When you're nervous, it's easy to get your mind set on simply plowing through everything you want to say as fast as you can, and the heck with whatever else is going on around you.

But, try instead, to **take a deep breath**, and think twice about what's really going on. You have a chance to build a strong relationship by how you spot and deal with these clues.

49. Offer MORE Options

It's funny. People like to choose. They like **options** to pick from.

Ask them if they want ice cream, and they say "No".

But ask them, instead, if they want a scoop of *vanilla or c* and *this* time, they quickly snap back with the flavor of th Yep, now, they *want* to buy ice cream!

Now, they've got to have it!

Why?

Because the "pitch" was framed as one of picking from **options**, rather than a flat out - yes or no.

And, there's the lesson: Take the time to think of where you could create choices, or options, for prospects to select from.

For example, in addition to listing a 5-day cleaning program in your proposal, show a 3-day **optional** cleaning program as well.

Or, how about rather than simply saying the customer will be responsible to provide the consumable poly/paper supplies, ask them if they would like to look at the **option** of having you track, order and restock these items for them, as an additional service.

Or, how about offering them an **optional** day cleaning version, as well as, the standard "after hours" version they're use to seeing.

They may have never considered it before, and may be interested, *even excited*, about this **option**... they had never thought of before.

Or, finally, how about having several **options** to choose from for each kind of extra service you provide, such as <u>carpet cleaning</u>, <u>tile maintenance</u>, <u>window cleaning</u>, etc.

For example, you could create three **optional** levels of service for carpet care, maybe Silver, Gold and Platinum.

Who <u>doesn't</u> like ordering from a menu?

50. What Makes A GREAT Presentation?

Well, YOU, of course.

Certainly, YOU and everything you bring to the presentation is important.

Attitude, Professionalism, Thoroughness, Attention To Detail.

All that's true; no doubt about it.

But today, we want to point out <u>one</u> thing you can do to move beyond a <u>good</u> presentation, and move in to the area of, as we said, making a GREAT presentation.

Here's the first part...

For your presentation to be great, you have to absolutely, without fail, make sure your prospect knows that...

YOU GET IT.

"Get what?" you may ask.

Well, they have to know you clearly understand everything about them and their situation, including:

- What cleaning problems they've gone through or are going through now.

- What they are looking for from the NEXT cleaning company to solve those problems.

It's so tempting for a cleaning contractor to think he or she has made a good presentation if they simply and politely deliver a professional looking proposal, review the various parts, and answer any questions the prospect has.

Well, it may, or may not, be good... but it certainly isn't great.

And that may be enough for most people, but it shouldn't be enough for someone who wants to be the best, like you!

It's actually just the start.

That's right, the real pros know their job is <u>much</u> more than simply being the "delivery" man for the bid. They know it's their job to make sure the prospect knows that they GET IT.

And how do they do that?

By listening and explaining, and then listening and explaining some more until the two of you... your prospect and you both, KNOW you're on <u>exactly</u> the "same page".

Let's see an example of what that would look like:

"In our first meeting, you made a comment about two issues you were having: Smear marks on the walls in the restrooms from mopping, as well as, areas of the building where the tile wasn't as shiny as you'd like to see."

"So, while measuring the building I noted any bathrooms that had the kinds of smear marks you were talking about, as well as, three areas where we saw the uneven appearance and shine of the tile."

Now, the second step is just as important. Here it is:

TIE IT TO A PLAN.

That's right, tie your answer to a plan.

So, in our example above, how could we tie the answer to a plan? Well, we could explain our plan as follows:

- We would schedule a crew our first week, to come in and wash down the restroom completely… so we can start off fresh.

- Then, we would train our nightly cleaning person to perform nightly spot cleaning of the walls every night, with more extensive wiping twice a month.

- We also would use a nightly checklist to keep track of the condition of the restrooms including the walls.

- And finally, every quarter, we would schedule a complete wall washing of all the restrooms.

Now, that's an example of taking your presentation to the "next level".

51. WHEN to Call Back

This is one of the most common questions we hear from cleaning companies about the bidding process. Here's why:

1. After so much work has gone into preparing a bid, no one wants to make a careless mistake right at the end that... *costs them the account!*

2. They worry about being too anxious, too eager and possibly... *scaring away the prospect.*

It's understandable.

But, you <u>shouldn't</u> feel ashamed of being eager to follow up and please your prospect. *To the contrary*, it's actually a very good thing you feel this way, because it shows... you care!

And that <u>is</u> important.

But, the thing is... we need to know <u>how</u> to present that caring attitude to our prospects in a way that <u>ATTRACTS</u> them, *rather than* <u>***scares***</u> *them away.*

So, we need to decide on a good rule of thumb for scheduling our follow ups for maximum results.

To help us do that, let's think back to another timing question you had to answer <u>before</u> you even got to this point:

How long did you wait after you completed your walk through of the building... before you called to set up a time and date to deliver the bid?

The answer, we hope, is a number of days that not only gave you the time you <u>needed</u>, but also reflected the kind of careful thought, effort and attention you <u>wanted</u> your prospect to KNOW went into preparing their bid.

Put it this way...

Have you ever seen an office cleaning quote simply *scratched* on the back of a business card saying something like... *"Price $285 - 2x/ week"*?

Well, we have.

And we know that card was simply left there on the desk after some cleaning contractor took maybe five minutes to look around!

Well, that's <u>not</u> the message you want to be sending to your prospects.

No prospect wants to feel <u>their</u> cleaning program **took 5 minutes to throw together!!!**

No, you want to wait a few days or more before you come back with a professional proposal ready to talk about with your prospect.

Well, it's the SAME in deciding how long to wait before "calling back" <u>after</u> delivering a proposal.

You want to give it an APPROPRIATE amount of time to allow your prospect to go over it carefully. They may need to review it with others in their company as well.

What's appropriate?

Well, of course, it depends.

If it's a large project, it may be appropriate to wait a week, or more, before calling back. It may easily take that long for them to get to it, get through it, and put together their questions.

If it's a small building, scheduled for cleaning only 1 or 2 times per week, you may be able to call back in as little as a couple days.

And of course, you should listen to your prospect for "clues" as to how urgently they want to review your bid.

As you can imagine, you should plan on "following up" a lot sooner with a building that just let their current cleaning company go, and are suddenly faced with having to cover the cleaning themselves, <u>versus</u> one that is simply going out to bid, to see "what's out there".

Ok, we won't dodge the bullet

What's a good rule of thumb?

In general, you should wait from <u>a couple days to a week</u>, depending on the size of the bid.

And, before we forget, if all else fails, there's always the secret, magical, hidden strategy of ... *simply asking the prospect!*

YOU: "Well, Steve, typically we give a client 2 or 3 days to go through everything before we call back. Do you think that would give you enough time?"

PROSPECT: "Sure, that should be fine."

YOU: "Ok then, if you have any questions in the meantime just give us a call, otherwise, we'll check back with you in a few days."

When you wait a while to call back your prospects to check on your bid you show <u>them</u> respect by giving them time to thoroughly review everything, while showing you're a busy professional as well. Win-Win.

P.S. By the way, we didn't even address the idea of waiting a long time to follow up with a prospect, or not at all, ... because... well, because it's just a bad idea.

52. WHAT To Say

Now, let's look at possibly an even more important question - "<u>What</u> should you say when you do call back?"

Hopefully by now, you're beginning to see a pattern develop in how to approach marketing and selling situations.

It's a pattern based on... **knowing your customer!**

Why?

Because, if we can <u>understand</u> our customer better than our competition, we can finally begin to work on creating a service matched to what they WANT, *rather than simply what we happen to have that day...*

So, let's see how "knowing our customer" answers a variety of other marketing and sales questions:

Our cover letter <u>shouldn't</u> be a short boring page about how great we are, but rather a crystal clear explanation of how we, more than any other cleaning contractor, understand their building, what they want, and how to consistently get it for them.

Our walk through...same thing! From taking detailed measurements and notes about every inch of their building to asking detailed questions about what they want from their cleaning service, it should be clear they are <u>not</u> just another bid to us.

Our bid presentation.... should always let our prospects know two important things:

First, that we understand or "GET THEM"; that we've been listening carefully to what they want. And two; that we've "TIED IT TO A PLAN" to make sure they get what they want.

QUESTION: What should you say when we call back?

ANSWER: All those things that reinforce the fact that you "get it" and have a way to "tie it to a plan" - to deliver the kind of cleaning they want.

(A review of your powerful Measurable Guarantees of Performance comes to mind here.)

You may also want to ask:

- If they've had any new questions come up from reviewing the program with <u>other</u> managers involved in the decision process.

- If the prices looked in order? ...in budget? Or did you need to sit down with them to re-work the tasks or frequencies.

- If, after having more time to review it, they <u>still</u> felt like the program addressed <u>all</u> the specifics you had discussed.

- If they had time to call any of your references, and did they have any questions from those conversations.

What else should you say during the follow up?

Well, certainly this is where selling styles differ.

Some folks would tell you to come out swinging, "asking for the sale", at some point saying something like "So, can we get the cleaning started for you next Monday, or would the first of the month be better?"

And, for some folks that may work fine.

But, our experience in the commercial cleaning industry has taught us to approach things a little differently.

You see, switching over your cleaning contractor can take time.

For one thing, changing the people who clean your building can be much more difficult than, for example, simply changing who you buy office supplies or copy toner from.

Plus, in cleaning, there are personalities, sometimes many personalities, involved.

Your competition and the person who they currently have working in the building may or may not be much of a cleaner, but either way, they may still have <u>very close personal ties</u> with the office staff.

So, we generally like the "soft sell" approach where we position ourselves as the professional consultant ready to "take care of things"- but when the <u>prospect's</u> ready... not necessarily when <u>we're</u> ready.

Remember: Our aim is to be next; the next company they go with when they decide to make the change.

53. Want REAL-Life Examples?

Ok, let's look at some "real life" suggestions of <u>what</u> to say when you give that all important "call back".

Ok, as in most things, having the right mindset is critical. So what should our mindset be?

Well, let's first describe what your mindset <u>shouldn't</u> be.

Here are the *thoughts* that shouldn't be going through your head when you're dialing the phone to follow up on one of your bids:

I hope our price is ok. I hope the proposal looked good. I hope they've called our references, checked with everyone they've needed to check with, and <u>are ready to give us the "go ahead" to start.</u>

Are you kidding?!

We can count on <u>one</u> hand the number of times in over 20 years, when we called to follow up on a bid and our prospective client said,

... "Oh, great, I'm so glad you called; I was <u>just</u> thinking about you. In fact, I've been meaning to call you to tell you everything looks great.

You're hired! And you can start anytime you'd like."

Yeah, <u>that</u> response comes about as often as this one,…

…*"We love your program, but your quote came in a little lower than the other cleaning companies, so, I was wondering if you'd like to raise the price… just to build in a little extra "cushion" for yourself."*

That's right… <u>not</u> often.

Maybe it's us… but a lot of times, here's how we found out we landed an account:

"Hey Dan, this is Steve at Acme Manufacturing, we've decided to go with you guys… when's the absolute soonest you could start because we let the other company go last night."

That's right, you wait and wait; then, out of the blue your new customer calls to see if you can start cleaning <u>immediately</u>.

So, we hope you're convinced by now that your prospect isn't sitting, *anxiously waiting by the phone*, thinking of you - hoping you'll call so they can award you the contract.

So, then what's the "follow up" call really about? Some people will tell you it's to push for the sale.

Not us.

We **want** them to **want** us, <u>not</u> to be "strong armed" into hiring us. So, here's our mind set when we make a follow up call.

We want our follow-up call to go something like this; not the exact words, but, the idea:

Hey there, prospective customer, it's us, the cleaning guys. We're busy like you, but not so busy to forget calling you back to check in.

When we left off last time, you were going to do some "homework" on your end such as checking references, talking to your boss or comparing prices etc.

We wanted to see how that went, and whether:

> (1). you have any other questions we need to get answered or hurdles we need to get through or

> (2). you were ready to set up a start date.

What we <u>don't</u> want to do is give the impression we've been thinking of them constantly and are desperate to hear whether or not they're going to hire us.

So, what comes across as interested but not needy? How's this:

"Hey Steve, this is Dave at ABC Commercial Cleaning. Before I headed out for appointments today, I had a note "pop up" on my computer reminding me to check in with you...and see how things were progressing as far as the cleaning proposal."

Note: This approach sends the message that while…

- they <u>are</u> important, and
- you <u>do</u> want their business, and
- you <u>are</u> interested in moving them towards a decision,

…You are NOT desperate.

Instead, it suggests your business, like theirs, is successful and that you're busy, like them...handling appointments, bidding etc...

In fact, it suggests that rather than anxiously waiting "counting the minutes" until they make a decision, a <u>scheduled computer note</u> simply *reminded* you to call them to follow up on their progress.

This approach does several important things:

1. It positions you as a busy, successful business person they'd like to do work with.

2. It shows them you are a professional and interested in being available for them to answer questions, but without putting pressure on them to decide <u>this minute</u>.

3. It gives them a gentle "poke in the ribs" to get moving on your proposal... if they've been dragging their heels.

By the way, here's what you'll often hear from the prospect when you use this approach:

"Oh, we're sorry Steve, things have been crazy here, and we just haven't had time to look at it."

To which we might respond....

"Steve, heck, don't even worry about it...I know how you feel... we've been growing like crazy here too!

In fact, that's kind of the reason I called. You see, we've got two new companies asking us to get them started the last two weeks of this month, and then a third one who wants to get going early next month, so the schedule coming up is looking awfully tight.

Since you were thinking of making a change pretty soon, I thought you might appreciate a heads up to see if you wanted me to try and hold that first week in August for you, rather than give it to that other company."

Now, **<u>that's</u>** different!

You'd be surprised how many times the prospect, who at first wasn't interested, changes their mind and quickly "gets interested".

And even if they don't "bite" on this opportunity, at least, they are left with the feeling you're viewed in the marketplace as "in demand" and "desirable" by at least several other businesses. (social proof!)

We'll talk more about this in the tip "Make 'Em Decide!" For now…

54. A WATCHED Pot Won't Boil

You've probably heard this expression before.

It could have been when you were nervously waiting to hear back about an important job interview, or maybe when one of your kids was anxiously waiting to hear if they "made" a sports team.

The "where" or "when" is less important than the "what" and "why", as in what does the expression mean and why is it so important for us to know when it comes to marketing and selling cleaning.

Well, WHAT the saying means, of course, is that it doesn't do any good to sit around fretting about something whose outcome is… out of your control.

You've put in the ingredients, and turned on the burner, *simply staring at the pot isn't going to help anything!*

In fact, it may actually hurt your chances of getting the desired result.

And, as far as the WHY, or more specifically, why this is important to know when you're selling cleaning programs; well, it's because of ENERGY!

Your energy

You only have so much of it to go around. So, rather than waste it, or lose it altogether, you need to direct it to where it can do the most good.

Too often, we hear from anxious cleaning contractors explaining they can't stop thinking about an account they've just bid on.

Desperately wanting to get the job, they endlessly run over and over in their minds what they should do next, whether they should call back again, when they should call back, and what they should say.

They're so anxious, so fixated on this account - they can think of little else. And it drains them of all their energy.

And that's the problem.

Fixated on landing any one account, they're immobilized, and as a result virtually stop moving forward on all the other potential jobs out there.

Now, we're not saying, don't do your scheduled follow up on every bid. You absolutely should!

What we are talking about is not letting any one account become so important in your mind, that you lose your energy and momentum on your other marketing efforts.

Schedule necessary follow up calls in your planner…and be done with it. That's right, until then, don't worry about it.

Remember, it's still a numbers game.

Do that, and watch your pot begin to boil.

55. MAKE 'Em Decide

You've done everything right. Everything seemed to go as planned, so…

Why haven't they called?

Yeah, why haven't they called to give you the "go ahead".

It can be maddening! What's the problem?

If you've been in the business any period of time, you know the answers (or excuses) can be endless, but typically they sound something like this....

"I still need to look it over a little bit more closely... before deciding." or

"I still have another manager to run it by... before we can make a final decision." or

"I'm still waiting for a couple more quotes to come in... before I can decide." or

"I was thinking of giving the current cleaning company once last warning... before making a change."

Some of these reasons (i.e. excuses, delays) may be legitimate. Many times they're not. Many times the reason they're not calling to give you the "go ahead" is......drum roll.

<u>Change</u>

People hate it. They say they don't, *but they do*.

Let's be honest. Generally, we all like to keep things pretty much the way they are.

And changing who will be in charge of cleaning your building. Well, that can be a <u>BIG</u> change.

It will force your prospect to do lots of things like:

- firing, letting go, dropping, terminating, releasing, or whatever term you want to use for the painful process of having to cancel the current cleaning service, which, by the way, many of their company's managers and employees may have gotten to know quite well over the years. *Ouch!*

- letting everyone who needs to know (bosses, managers, security etc.) that one cleaning company is leaving and a new one is starting. *Ugh!*

- making arrangements with the "old" cleaning contractor when their last day will be.

- getting the keys back from the "old" cleaning company

- issuing those same keys to the "new" cleaning company

- assigning all new security codes for the "new" cleaning company

- orienting the "new" cleaning company to their building and its safety and security procedures.

That's a <u>lot</u> of change.

And it can be a real aggravation for your prospective client. You try to make it as easy and seamless as possible...but it's still a pain.

So, <u>that</u> can be part of the reason why your phone isn't ringing.

Ok, makes sense, but is there anything you can do to get your prospective client to "quit dragging their heels"... and hire you?

Here are three specific strategies to get your prospects to quit "sitting on their hands" and pick up the phone to hire you.

The first strategy is...

Give them an INCENTIVE !!

In other words... give them a reason to decide NOW, rather than later.

An old tried and true business rule says, "Reward <u>that</u> which you want done!"

So, for example, if you want salespeople to sell the new models of stoves at the appliance store... you could offer them a special, high commission, on every one of the new models they sell!

And when you do, sit back and watch as the salespeople suddenly start to sell the new model stoves.

It's simply human nature. You can try to fight it... but you'll likely lose. So, what kind of an incentive could you offer to strongly motivate them to decide to make a change?

Well, here's a couple examples of what you could offer to "make 'em decide":

- FREE stripping and refinishing of all of their waxable tile... if they call back <u>within</u> 2 weeks of you delivering the proposal to schedule a start date.

Or

- FREE initial cleaning of all office areas... if they call back <u>within</u> 2 weeks of your delivering the proposal, to arrange a mutually convenient start date for the cleaning program.

You get the idea - a compelling incentive, or reason, to make the change. Here's the second strategy:

Give them a DEADLINE!

That's right, when you give a restriction on how long an offer is good for, you create two very important things:

1. a sense of URGENCY, and

2. a fear of LOSS

And those two "things" can get your prospects to take action NOW, rather than later.

Finally, here's a third strategy to get your prospects to make up their minds and take action...

Offer a LIMITED supply!

That's right, when you promote a <u>limited</u> supply of something, anything, you naturally "fuel the flames" of your buyers desire for your product or service.

- The appeal of the Mona Lisa isn't just that it's a "nice" painting... it's also that there's <u>only</u> <u>one</u>.

- The appeal of front row seats isn't just that they're super comfortable seats... it's that there's <u>so</u> <u>few</u>.

Create a limited supply of spots available for "taking on new clients" in your cleaning business, and you may have just found an effective way to turn prospects into customers!

56. FIND Reasons to Stop By

You may have heard the expression, "Give yourself the gift of a good habit!" Well, here's one gift you should seriously look at giving yourself....

Get in the habit of "finding" reasons to stop back to see your prospects. Whether it's...

- having to stop back to get a couple measurements you missed on you first walk-through... or

- having to drop off a couple recently updated certificates of insurance… or

- having to show them some sales literature showing pictures of the latest time saving equipment you use.. or

- having to drop off the MSDSs on the set of "green" products you use.

The reason you stop back out <u>isn't</u> as important as cultivating the habit of making a point of getting back into the building to "touch base" with your prospects.

Now, we're <u>not</u> talking of being too needy or prospect "stalking" here. What we <u>are</u> talking about, however, is orchestrating intentional visits designed to give you a chance to interact with your prospect.

The goal of which is to develop a <u>closer</u> relationship than…

…just someone who measured their building, <u>one</u> time, <u>one</u> day, for <u>one</u> hour!

The reason you give simply provides a harmless "excuse" or reason to see your prospect again.

This strategy just "happens" to give you yet another chance to "visit" <u>without</u> them feeling pressured.

Plus, you can earn your prospect's respect when you "happen" to pop in now and then to give them something that's cleaning related and that you think they'd be interested in seeing; or to take care of something work related, like updating their cleaning proposal etc.

Becoming comfortable seeing you around and "visiting" with you... can often turn into liking and trusting you.

Your visits don't have to be long. Give it a try. The more you do it... the easier it becomes.

INSIDER SECRET #5
WORKLOAD The Work:
The CleanBid Program

57. Why Price Per Square Foot WON'T Fly

Could a simple price per square foot approach work when bidding on office-cleaning jobs?

Maybe.

Yeah, <u>maybe</u> if all cleaning companies were the same, it *might* work. But they're not!

And, <u>maybe</u> if all customers wanted the same thing, it *might* work.

But, they don't.

And there's the rub.

See, broad, one-size-fits-all approaches to bidding office-cleaning like *price per square foot*, <u>might</u> work, if all cleaning companies were all the same size, cleaned the same, had the same costs, and expected the same profit.

But they <u>don't</u>.

The really big ones <u>may</u> come close.

Really large cleaning companies, some of whom, may have 500, 1000, or more employees... may come close.

At <u>that</u> level, the "players" (competing cleaning contractors) may begin to look *similar*; similar management structure, similar approaches to cleaning, similar quality control methods, and maybe most importantly... similar expense ratios and profit requirements.

And at <u>that</u> level of play, per square foot based pricing <u>may</u> work adequately.

But, the reality is the vast majority of cleaning businesses don't look <u>anything</u> like that.

No, the truth is <u>most</u> cleaning companies vary greatly in:

- How they CLEAN - one person, area, or "team" cleaning

- How LARGE they are - from one person to a hundred or more.

- What KIND of cleaning they offer - from straight janitorial, office- cleaning to residential, ...to any number of other types, such as carpet or industrial cleaning.

- What their OVERHEAD, or PROFIT requirements are.

And those differences... *make a difference!*

That's right, for most cleaning companies...

Figuring out what price to charge for office-cleaning should <u>start</u> with figuring out... the TIME.

And what TIME is that?

Well, it's the estimate for how long it should take, on average, to clean the building.

The reason we say, *on average*, is, we all know, things come up that may take a little longer to do than usual some nights, or may save a little time on others.

But, that's <u>not</u> the point.

The point is when you start with a good *estimate*, or average, of how long a building will take to clean... you've got a lot!

And when you start with THAT, you're <u>miles ahead</u> of the guy who decides on his monthly price by either dividing the total sq. ft. by some arbitrary production rate, or by multiplying it by some just as arbitrary price per sq. ft. figure.

Over-simplified measures give over-simplified answers.

And over-simplified answers in a business like cleaning, can quickly turn around to <u>bite</u> you in the form of under-priced jobs which leads to lower profits. To avoid this, we recommend you:

Workload each office-cleaning job you're bidding on!

For our purposes, *workloading* is the process of using specific information about a building such as floor measurements (i.e. room dimensions), floor types (i.e. carpet, tile) and fixture counts (sinks, toilets) along with a schedule of job specifications where each cleaning task has an associated production rate per sq. ft. or by item count, to calculate an average cleaning time.

Yes, there's a lot to it. But, fortunately, there's help available to make it easy, a whole lot easier, ...more about that later.

For now, it's important to realize how critical it is to <u>start</u> with calculating a cleaning time for office cleaning, and <u>then</u> set the price... *not the other way around!*

Ok, let's cut to the chase.

As you may or may not know, we have our own online tool - the CleanBid Janitorial Program at **www.CleanBid.net**, to help on bidding office-cleaning projects, and yes, we think it's terrific for doing everything you need - from calculating cleaning times and getting monthly prices to getting a professional looking proposal.

But, you don't have to use it.

<u>Really</u>, we mean it, you don't. If you have another way of work-loading buildings efficiently when you bid... great! No hard feelings.

The <u>important</u> thing is that one way or another, you <u>do</u> workload them! That's right, you'll be way ahead of the game if you calculate an average cleaning time before deciding on a price when you bid on janitorial, office-cleaning jobs.

How? Well, it's this....

-Get away from guessing cleaning times and monthly prices, and

-Get away from simply setting your price *close* to whatever the prospect *says* they're paying now. (hint; *this may come as a shock,* but they may <u>not</u> always be telling you the whole truth)

Instead, do what the winners do... workload them! A great deal of our success in the commercial, office-cleaning business can be credited to this one idea. It makes sense... *and it makes cents!*

58. MEASURE Twice - Cut Once

Ever had to drive out to a building to measure different areas to figure out how much to charge for a carpet cleaning or tile stripping and refinishing job?

Ever had to go back a second... or third time?

It can happen. And it used to happen to us, until we discovered a way to nearly eliminate this time-wasting problem completely.

But, here's what we eventually learned:

To discipline ourselves to take the time to measure <u>properly</u>, <u>thoroughly</u> and <u>accurately</u>... **the first time!**

And if we were uncertain of a measurement during that first walk-through - we'd measure it again before leaving - not leaving until we were confident we got it right.

That's right, during the initial walk-through, we'd slow things down, to make sure we get only the most accurate information possible to load into the bidding program.

NOW, the good news is, when you take the time to create an accurate list, showing the breakout of size and floor type - by area, you'll have in your hands an incredible reference tool to help you do <u>two</u> important things:

1. Create an accurate and professional proposal.

PLUS...

2. Calculate prices for "project work" or "one-time job" requests (like carpet cleaning or tile stripping and refinishing), quickly and easily.

Then, when the last minute "call" comes in from one of your regular office cleaning customers asking for you to quote them a price to strip and refinish the hallways and lunchroom over the phone, you'll be able to quickly "pull out" your list of building information, and instantly know the size and floor type of every area of the building.

And, something just as important, *as long as they haven't had any remodeling*, you'll be able to <u>trust</u> your measurements are "good".

And that's important, because when you're not <u>sure</u>, you know what happens...

That's right, you, or someone in your company has to make a <u>separate</u> trip out to that building to re-measure ... just so you can finally, really, be sure.

What a waste of time and gas!

Time that could have been used for any number of things like marketing, training, inspecting or selling etc..

59. Competitive & Credible: The One - Two PUNCH!

You see it all the time.

You go out to meet the person in charge of hiring the janitorial, office-cleaning for a building.

It can be *Grumpy Gary*, the general manager at an auto dealership or *Bored Brenda* the office supervisor at an insurance company.

It doesn't matter which.

If our Gary or Brenda are unhappy with their cleaning, or just "going out for bids", here's an almost guaranteed way to get these *grumpy or bored* prospects <u>excited</u> about your cleaning company.

Bring them something competitive & credible! **It's as simple, and as difficult, as that.**

What do we mean?

Well, the simple part is, that it's so simple to understand, isn't it?

When it comes to being competitive, as we've said, it's pretty clear to nearly everyone by now that cleaning budgets have never been watched more closely!

And just pretending it doesn't matter - won't work.

And as far as being credible, we think we all also understand that you can deliver the most competitive bid in the world, but if the prospect doesn't believe you can actually deliver what you promising... you're sunk!

Oh, by the way, let's go back to competitive again. We want to be clear about something.

We <u>didn't</u> say lowest price, we said competitive!

And there's a big difference. We never played the "We're the cheapest guys in town" game and suggest you don't either.

It's a losing strategy as far as we're concerned.

No, instead, we suggest being competitive. And competitive, to our way of thinking, means "reasonable considering what they're getting for the money."

Again, we're talking VALUE!

So, if you're offering a high quality service, you need to be priced accordingly.

Interestingly enough, many cleaning contractors would be surprised to learn how often the "higher price for higher quality" guy <u>outperforms</u> the "lowest possible price" guy!

60. Dip Your Toe In FIRST!

To explain what we mean here, let us tell you how those words saved us a small fortune...*and may someday do the same for you!*

You see, one day one of our managers sat down to "vent" about a frustrating problem. It seems a customer had asked for a price on removing from a concrete factory floor, what appeared to be years of built up grease, grime, and who knows what else!

It was bad.

And our manager couldn't seem to figure out how to price the job. "I mean", as he put it, "How in the world do we know how long it's going to take, or for that matter, even if the "stuff" will come off, or how it's going to look when we're done!?"

He made a good point.

And you've probably run across one or two of these kinds of *oddball,* tricky, and sometimes potentially disastrous jobs. And if you haven't yet, chances are you will!

So what can you do? Well, let's look at our problem a little closer.

Well, first, the customer had added to the problem by dropping the pricing "hot potato" in our lap saying something like,

"Oh, and we need a total price for what it's going to cost... you know, one price for the <u>whole</u> job."

Well, here's the rub; normal rates for cleaning tasks like floor scrubbing can quickly go 'out the window' when trying to estimate times and prices for these kinds of jobs.

And worse yet, because of the questionable condition of the floor, we were not only unsure of how to price the job, we were also concerned how it was going to look when we were done!

And remember, the only thing worse, from a customers perspective, than paying too much for a job is paying too much for a job.....they <u>don't like</u> when you're done!

So, here's an idea:

Consider offering to do a small 'test patch' for FREE, or "at cost", or some minimum amount; it's up to you.

See, when you do a 'test patch'; which is basically a closet here or a 'hardly-ever-used' hallway there, you get a chance to safely learn the answer to two important questions:

One - based on this 'test patch' how hard is this job going to be?

Two - after our best efforts, what can the customer expect the results to look like?

Two important answers to know

Now, back to the story...in our case, we did just a very small area, maybe 20 feet in an inconspicuous spot in the plant.

And, boy, did we quickly learn how long the floor was going to take... short answer - FOREVER!

At least, that's the way it seemed. Yeah, it was overwhelming!

But, **we "dodged" the bullet of getting locked into doing this job**, by using the "Dip Your Toe In First!" strategy.

That's right, because after the customer saw how the "test patch" looked ... he realized even our best efforts weren't going to save this old plant floor.

They may have to leave it alone for now and have it resurfaced and/or resealed one day, but for now, at least, they decided it just wasn't worth the time or money!

***Whew!* We breathed a long sigh of relief**......

You may be wondering, "Why not propose to do the whole thing time & materials?" instead.

Well, again, this customer wasn't interested in signing on to an open ended, hourly rate plus materials arrangement.

If the customer would have been willing to let us work under those conditions, it could have worked... but we probably would have had them "sign off" on the work along the way.

Oh, and maybe even pay for the work along the way too!

But, the real value of this strategy is simply having a way to deal with unpredictable cleaning challenges in a way that shows your professionalism and willingness to help, but not in a reckless or potentially costly way.

Your customer will be able to see you don't want to waste their money or your time, on something that may, or may not, give them the kind of results they're looking for.

61. EXTREMELY Profitable Jobs: The Double Edged Sword!

How in the world can we say that?

How could having extremely profitable accounts be anything but great news!

Ok, well, let us explain by asking a series of questions.

First, do you think anyone else would like to get a hold of your highly profitable accounts?

Yep, your competition is no doubt lurking close by "licking their chops" and would like nothing better than to swoop in and pick up all your best jobs.

Second, do you think those competitors are sitting back quietly or do you think they are bombarding your best clients asking to submit a bid ASAP?

Yeah, they're probably *falling all over themselves*, lining up asking to bid against you at many of your accounts... all the time.

Third, in the world we compete in today, do you think the bids are coming in more often on the insanely high side... or the ridiculously low side?

Yeah, if your city is anything like ours, bids are coming in *lean and mean*.

Finally, are your business customers feeling *footloose and fancy free*, or under enormous pressure to cut costs and save money anywhere they can?

Ok, we're not even going to answer this one, because you already <u>know</u> the answer.

So, now can you understand why we suggest that highly profitable accounts are a *mixed* bag?

That's right, on one hand, we love having the account and we're certainly glad it's profitable, but what we of course don't love, is the vulnerability it exposes us to in a competitive marketplace.

We don't want to ever live under the "illusion" that simply because our company delivers reliable, quality janitorial services, we can get away thinking for even a minute that...*things couldn't change!*

No, we <u>know</u> better... maybe you do too.

So, what do you do?

Well, we wouldn't have you go out and recklessly slash your prices on your highly profitable accounts anytime soon simply because you're feeling vulnerable.

But here's what we do recommend...

You should deliver cleaning services whose quality and reliability justify your prices being in the "upper range" of "competitive".

That's right, we suggest aiming to be among the higher priced bidders... of the proposals, from quality companies, considered "competitive".

Now, there are exceptions to this "shoot for the high side of middle" pricing strategy.

For example, if your cleaning company can offer services in either quality or personal attention <u>unlike</u> any of your competitors... then by all means price accordingly. (Note: We'll talk about this later in Insider Secret #6: Deliver NOTICE-able Cleaning!")

That's right; in this best-of-all-cases scenario, you can demand higher premium prices and rightfully expect to get them because you're delivering a premium service.

And that's a good thing.

62. ALL Things Aren't Equal

Have you ever had a customer cut back?

We know, silly question; because nearly everyone who has run a cleaning business for any length of time has likely experienced this situation, and probably more than once.

The call may have sounded something like this….

"We need to cut our cleaning expense in half, so we need to reduce our service from 6 days a week to 3 days right away."

Well, be careful!

….. All things aren't equal.

Yes, our customers went through ups and downs over the years, like all companies do, and sometimes that meant having to cut back on services… including cleaning.

And when they called, they often had it in their mind that the **price of cleaning should be exactly proportionate to the frequency**.

Well, it's not, at least not very often

For example, if they're paying $300/ month for twice per week cleaning, they may be convinced they should only have to pay $150 for once per week.

Their thinking being: half the visits, half the price.

The problem is when is comes to the hours, expenses, profit and price, you can't just adjust proportionally, at least, not if you hope to end up making an appropriate profit.

It just doesn't work that way.

Without getting too detailed, here's the problem in a nutshell...

...If you cut the price in half for a customer who's reducing the frequency of their cleaning in half, you may be left <u>barely</u> making a profit, or possibly only covering your costs.

Why?

Well, several reasons:

First, when you clean only once a week, you'll generally arrive to find the building dirtier than if you were stopping out to visit twice per week.

And if it takes slightly longer to clean on a once a week schedule, let's say 4 ½ vs. 4 hrs./visit, you can quickly see how cutting the price by half (a full 50%), can leave you coming up short when it comes to profit!

Second, large monthly bills often have smaller profit margins built in than smaller ones.

And, if you cut the price in half for half the number of days, you may have inadvertently lowered the actual profit margin, or percentage, to an unacceptably low level for your business.

Solution?

When a customer has to go through cut-backs on services like cleaning, always work up a reasonable "new price", for the reduced program, <u>rather</u> than automatically agreeing to a proportionate price reduction.

Estimate the number of hours of cleaning you might need for the reduced schedule, and then calculate a fair price to cover your expenses and necessary profit.

As the saying goes...

It's "Ready-**Aim**-Fire", <u>NOT</u> "Ready- **Fire** -Aim"!

63. We Make It Up In VOLUME?

"We lose a little bit on every job... but we make it up in volume!"

Have you ever heard <u>that</u> line before?

It's supposed to be funny.

And it is, if you realize it's highlighting one of the most <u>ridiculous</u> business strategies ever.... the idea that making money on each job isn't important as long as...*you're doing lots of them!*

We know, it sounds *crazy*, and it <u>would</u> be funny, if it wasn't for the fact that so many hard-working cleaning businesses run their business...as if it were true!

We hope you're not one of them, but if you are - don't despair!

That's right, you should start moving in the direction of having all, or nearly all (*we'll talk about exceptions later*) of your accounts making money.

So, how do you do that?

Well, here's where the "heavy lifting" comes in.

You need to take and review a financial "snapshot" of each of your accounts regularly, <u>at least</u> monthly - to see how profitable or unprofitable they are.

You may have accounting and time-keeping software that helps you do this, or you may simply have to pull together the sales and expense data on your own to see if you're making money...and, if so, how much. But...

Be ready for some surprises!

You'll have them; we all do.

There are the accounts you think are great, but when you look at them, you find you're really losing money... when you consider <u>all</u> your expenses.

Then, there are the *quiet* accounts you call to check in with, but otherwise you never hear a *peep* from. There not real big or flashy, but, it turns out they're some of your <u>profit champions</u>!

Now, we're not saying dump the big accounts you found were losing money for a month or two. And we're not saying, that a small account that happens to be showing great profits for a while... is on auto-pilot either.

Nope, it's <u>not</u> that simple.

No, real business success requires <u>paying attention</u>. Not once, but regularly. The same thing holds true for profitability.

You want to make good financial decisions. But to do that you need the facts.

In fact, that's job 1 - Getting good information.

And then, you can begin to think about what it means, so you can make good financial decisions.

That may mean a number of things.

It may mean doing nothing, and simply watching the reports a few more months to see if something is a "trend" or a "fluke"

Sometimes, even a great account can lose money for a while, for example, when you're first starting to get it up and running.

You'll often need to think about whether a lack of profitability is temporary or the sign of bigger problems, such as an ongoing history of being unable to stay within the budgeted cleaning hours assigned to the account.

- It may mean adjusting the budgeted hours at one account, while sitting down to ask for a raise at another.

- It may even mean dropping an account or two if you can't find a way to turn the financial picture around.

But whatever it ends up meaning to you, it should be based on first gathering and reviewing good financial information.

Now, there can be *exceptions* to this rule.

For example, you may clean one small office once a week at breakeven, or maybe even a loss, it you are making healthy profits at three other large buildings you clean for the same client.

You may find the total profit to be acceptable.

Or you may not make as much as you'd like on your monthly general cleaning with another customer, but you allow it because you do "really well" on handling their "extra" project work like tile and carpet jobs.

But again, these are exceptions, and the main thing is to make those decisions with your "financial eyes" wide open.

64. We're In BUDGET

No doubt about it, it sure is exciting to announce to the office you've just "landed a new account!"

Making a sale is, and always will be, a thrill.

But, there's something just as important that you don't generally find people running around the office boasting about.

But they should.

And that's getting, and keeping, those accounts "in budget".

That's right, once you land an account, one of your first priorities should be assigning it the "budgeted hours" you used to determine the monthly price.

Those are simply the hours per night you can "safely" spend each visit to clean the account.

Stay "in budget" and you're on track to make money month after month. Start going "over your budget" with any regularity and you'll soon find you're managing, staffing, cleaning and inspecting an account... you're losing money at!

It's that simple. It's that important.

Let's take a look.

Say, an account was bid at 6 hours a night, and you or your staff start spending 7 or 8 hours each visit; well, the new account you were so proud of, could quickly become a profit "dog".

Any exceptions? Sure.

When you first start an account up, it'll take longer to get it "up to snuff" and for your folks to get used to cleaning it.

And even after you've had an account running smoothly there will still be nights, now and then, when you run over on your time for one reason or another - such as a pizza party cleanup, or preparations for a big VIP visit.

But those exceptions need to be just that - exceptions.

Generally, the hours should be pretty steady - right around the budgeted hours you assigned to the account.

You should consistently watch the hours you're spending cleaning on a regular basis and move quickly to investigate and take corrective steps if cleaning times start running high.

Those corrective steps can range all the way from a conversation to remind the cleaning associate to "stay in budget", to a complete re-training of the account to make sure everything is being done properly and efficiently.

Again, it's not as 'fun' as "landing an account" but it's just as important and can be just as financially rewarding.

Ever heard the old saying about the connection between the money you earn and the money you actually end up with, that goes...

"It's not what you make ...it's <u>what</u> <u>you</u> <u>keep</u>!"

Well, when it comes to this topic, the saying could be expressed in a similar way, "It's not the accounts you land, it's the accounts you keep in budget!"

65. What's MORE Important - Sales Or Profits?

The SALES camp would say, you can't spend what you don't have ....
and you don't have <u>anything</u> until you make a sale.

That sounds right. *Right?*

Now, the PROFIT camp would say you can't spend sales, only profits...
and the only thing that's <u>really</u> yours is the profit.

Yeah, that makes sense too.

So, which is it?

And the answer is ..., drum roll please.... neither! As in NEITHER is <u>more</u>
important than the other, and BOTH, as in they are both <u>very</u> important.

Sorry

Yes, like most of the answers to questions in the real world, the answer
isn't always, in fact, *hardly ever is,* black or white.

The truth lies somewhere in the murky middle.

But, if you look hard to find your answers in that murky middle, you'll
discover answers that are not only ok, but, are in fact, very powerful.

So, let's take a look...SALES first.

You know we preach to never stop marketing. And we stand by that.

But, what, you may ask, is so bad about an on-again, off-again marketing
approach?

Well, at best, you'll have accounts coming in now and then, "feast
or famine".

But, in the worst case, you could get caught "with your pants down", if you were to lose several accounts, or one big one - leaving you scrambling with no more in the "pipeline" to replace it.

Now what about PROFITS?

Well, making a profit is one of the things that virtually defines you as a business. Anything else may be a hobby, charity, or promising idea... *but not a business!* At least, not one you'll be running very long.

So, yes, we're <u>serious</u> about making profits... and suggest you be serious about it as well.

And our biggest suggestion regarding both sales and profits is this ... *pay attention*!

That's right, there are a lot of things you can grow quickly and run profitably, but it all starts with paying attention.

So, let's get right down to it.

You pick up a new account... and the budget you assign to it is, let's say, 6 hrs. per night.

If you make the proper level of profit at 6 hours a night in an account, well, then, if you start seeing 8 hrs. being spent every visit... there's <u>something</u> wrong <u>somewhere</u>!

We don't know what it is... but "there's a fungus among us!" and you better PAY ATTENTION and find out what it is, and correct it.

Because if you don't.... well, you know as well as we do... *no one else will.*

And this "paying attention" thing goes for more expenses than just payroll. Here's another example, and then we promise to get off our "soap box".

There was a dumpster in a parking lot of a medical building near our office.

And for months, maybe over a year, we drove by and saw that thing filled to the brim, in fact, often overflowing with people's garbage that we could safely assume did <u>not</u> come from that building.

It appeared that everyone in the world had been throwing all kinds of trash into that dumpster, including nearby lawn care companies that filled it with their grass cuttings.

Why do we tell you this story?

Because that building had been throwing hundreds, if not, thousands of dollars down the drain by having to have that big dumpster emptied … simply because they were not paying attention to what was going on.

Well, finally, one day, we saw they switched to a dumpster with a lockable lid. And finally, for the first time, there was no one else's garbage to be seen in the dumpster but their own.

All we could think was - …. _about time!_

The secret to both sales and profits isn't a secret at all…but rather something as simple as PAYING ATTENTION.

66. We're Doing More Work… Why AREN'T We Making More Money?

Ever felt that way?

Ever wondered why it seems you're cleaning more accounts than ever, but <u>not</u> making any more money?

In fact, ever feel like you're barely making the <u>same</u> as when you had to handle <u>fewer</u> jobs?!

How can this be? *It's enough to drive you nuts!*

You "<u>know</u>" you're bidding them the same. At least, you <u>think</u> you are. That can't be it, can it?

So, what the heck is going on?!

Well, it might come down to one thing.... OVERHEAD.

What's that? What is overhead?

Well, ask a hundred people and you'll likely get a hundred different answers. But, for today, simply think of overhead as all of your expenses, other than, or on top of, wages and payroll taxes.

So, we're talking about things like cleaning chemicals, rent, utilities, gasoline, and any training, managerial or administrative office wages or salaries NOT already covered by the direct wages of any individual account.

Overhead is an expense category that's normally shown as a percentage in order to calculate how much each account needs to "kick in", or contribute, to pay for all expenses other than direct wages and payroll taxes.

Basically, each job or account you clean needs to "pay" its fair share of the total overhead expense (fixed and variable).

It's a little hard to "get your head around this" at first, but it's important, because overhead, or more specifically, not accurately accounting for overhead, is

....<u>where the trouble can start!</u>

Specifically, when you:

1. Don't account for all of your <u>current</u> expenses, or

2. Don't account for <u>new</u> expenses coming in such as:

    -buying new equipment

    -hiring new managers

    -bringing on new office help

    -buying a new computer or phone system

    -spending more on gasoline or repairs....

You can be headed for trouble!

All of these factors can increase your overhead, and if you haven't accounted for them in your pricing, you may begin to feel like … "You're doing more work...but not making any more money!"

Here's what's happening:

You may be calculating your prices using some simple method you've always used, which simply multiplies the hours *you think* it will take, by some hourly rate *you think* is fair.

But, that hourly rate may <u>not</u> reflect the fact that things have changed.

Your old way of setting an hourly rate to charge may not be taking into account certain <u>new expenses,</u> such as the hiring of a new HR Mgr., purchasing of a new phone system, or simply the increasing cost for things like gasoline or supplies.

So, it's very often these changes (increases) in overhead that cleaning businesses tend to temporarily ignore, or miss altogether.

Let us tell you a story...

Years ago, we were humming along, thinking everything was going great. We were quickly picking up accounts and starting them just as fast.

Wonderful, right?

Wrong.

We kept running into a problem month after month.

When we looked at how we priced each job, it <u>looked</u> like <u>each</u> account was making money, but our P & L wasn't showing the same profit, *not even close! And,*

We sure <u>weren't</u> seeing it in our checking account!

Why?

Well, because, at that point, we had not yet begun to accurately factor in overhead when calculating prices.

We had set an overhead percentage of let's say 35% of labor, but when we really looked at all of our expenses, it turned out the overall overhead percentage needed to be more LIKE 50% to cover everything.

That's a big difference. In our case, it was the difference between making money and losing money!

Ouch! Now what?

Well, we eventually created a proprietary, <u>sliding scale approach</u> to assigning overhead to each bid. It's this same sliding scale approach we use today for calculating overhead, as well as profit percentage, in our CleanBid Program.

But, no matter how you bid your jobs, you need to be looking at having each account pay its "fair share" of the overhead.

175

To get back to our story, when we finally applied the correct (higher) overhead to our P&L calculations... well, you can just imagine how each account's profitability looked!?

Yeah, pretty bad.

But, for the first time... more realistic. They finally reflected what was really going on.

It was a wake up call.

And the good news is:

- -We survived. We learned to accurately account for all of our expenses when we priced new jobs or went back to look at any existing account's "real" profitability.

- -We learned a way to have each account pay its "fair share" of the total bill.

- -We increased prices on some current accounts, and started to bid higher on new jobs, to account for covering these very real overhead expenses.

Only then did we find <u>real</u> and <u>lasting</u> profitability. You can too!

67. Use MINIMUMS to Protect Your Bottom Line

Today, all you seem to hear about is the power of maximums.

Maximum Speed! Maximum Returns! Maximum Protection!

Well, we're here to tell you about the power of <u>minimums</u> - like <u>minimum</u> frequencies, <u>minimum</u> profit per month and <u>minimum</u> number of hours!

Let's look at them one at a time.

First, minimum FREQUENCIES. Look at setting up a minimum frequency (number of cleaning visits per week) in order for you to consider cleaning a building is a good idea.

Why?

Well, let's just say this...landing a one-time per week account may be easy. But, that may be the only easy part. That's right, getting it filled and keeping it filled with a competent cleaner...is more of a challenge!

Sure, there are lots of places looking at one time per week cleaning. And, yes, you can always, we suppose, try to schedule several of them together creating some sort of "route".

You don't have to convince us.

Heck, we tried it off and on for years. But for us, in the end, it just proved to be too difficult and too fragile an arrangement to build a growing and profitable cleaning company with.

So, we set minimums. First we decided we would not take on any new account where the cleaning frequency was less than 2 (two) times per week; only to find ourselves later on increasing the minimum to 3 (three) times per week.

Your minimum can be different... but you should, at least, have one.

Second, minimum PROFITS. Setting up a minimum dollar amount you need to make per job, per month.

That's right, if the dollars of profit made using a percentage method fall below a certain amount - we required a minimum profit instead.

So, for example, on the Price Generator section of our CleanBid

Janitorial Program, if the monthly profit using the percentage method came in at only $83, we turned to a minimum profit method instead, where we required any job to give us a profit of no less than, let's say $125 or $135.

And, as far as one-time jobs are concerned... you may want to set up even higher minimums. You may want, for example, to never accept less than $175 or $200 profit on a one-time job.

Third, minimum NUMBER OF HOURS. Here, we're looking at setting up a minimum number of cleaning hours per visit any account needed to have, in order for you to consider bidding on it.

For example, how will you staff and keep staffed an account requiring only one hour of cleaning per visit!

Not easily, that's how.

It isn't that we want you to turn away business. The point is, however, all business isn't created equal.

And, of course, the main reason for looking at setting up minimums is to focus on getting the kind of stable accounts you will be able to staff and clean successfully, without slowing down your ability to keep growing.

Put simply: Use minimums so you can grow at maximum speed ...and profitability!

PART III
HOW TO KEEP

INSIDER SECRET #6
Deliver NOTICE-able Cleaning

68. DELIGHT Your Customers

How can you deliver cleaning that **delights** your customer - at prices that delight you?

Now that's a question worth finding an answer to, wouldn't you agree? And to find the answer, we need to look at the two parts of the question separately.

First, what kind of cleaning delights a customer?

Here are some examples...

- -When they see their offices right after you've taken on the building and have completed the initial cleaning.

- -When they walk in to see the waxable tile in the building has been completely stripped and refinished.

- -When they come in on a Monday morning to find all the carpeting has been completely cleaned and deodorized.

And what is the common factor in all of these situations? It's this...

They NOTICE the cleaning.

It looks different - it's <u>NOTICEABLE!</u>

Well, of course, you might say... that's obvious. So, why are we taking all this time to point it out? Well, think about this for a minute...

Is it possible that much of what determines whether a customer will be delighted with any cleaning company's service depends to a great deal on this one factor alone....

...whether or not they NOTICE it?

We declare a clear and forceful "YES!"; and suggest that our answer shouldn't really surprise anyone too much..

Isn't it really just "human nature"?

And, we know how powerful that is! It's that same human nature that explains why our moment of <u>greatest</u> joy in receiving a gift is generally felt... *just as we're ripping off the paper and opening the box...*

...only to be <u>quickly</u> followed by less and less "delight", as we soon lose our interest in it altogether, tossing it aside with the other gifts we're now somehow "bored" of.

It's crazy; it's sad, and one might even say shameful.

And we wouldn't even bring it up other than it's true. And we can learn from it.

Have you ever found yourself saying something like, "Boy, they (the customer) sure loved us when we <u>first</u> took over the cleaning. Yep, they really noticed how much we improved everything in the beginning, and told us so!"

"Now that some time has passed, even though we keep *busting our butt* out there, we hardly hear a peep... other than to call to say we missed something."

What's going on here?

Could it be that...

Even a very good cleaning company can become "invisible", taken for granted, and not appreciated over time, if they're not careful?

Yes; but, it <u>doesn't</u> have to be this way... at least, not for you.

Think about this question.

How can we combat this problem and instead, turn around and use this revolutionary discovery about what "delights" our customers, to create a winning and profitable strategy for landing and keeping cleaning accounts?

In other words, how can you intentionally, creatively and consistently **<u>create</u>** more of these "moments of delight" for your customer?

Put yet another way...

How can you create an actual, workable, practical strategy to create a steady stream of "moments" when customers NOTICE the cleaning... and become delighted?

Powerful questions; well, here's <u>our</u> answer...

69. Deliver <u>NOTICE</u>-able Cleaning!

But how? Well, here's two important ways:

1. By creating a clear DIFFERENCE in the cleaning; a noticeable "before and after" effect.

2. By using a REMINDER, or series of reminders which make your customer keenly <u>aware</u> that you and your cleaning people were definitely there last night!

Take a minute to let that really sink in.

We need to create a way of consistently delivering a series of NOTICE-able cleaning experiences for our clients.

"Sure, but how?"

Well, here are some examples:

1. Create a **<u>schedule</u>** consisting of touch-up or light cleaning(s) followed by an intensive, NOTICE-able, "shot-in-the-arm" type detail cleaning.

2. On each visit (light <u>and</u> detail) have a **number of techniques or methods** intentionally designed to make it perfectly obvious (NOTICE-able) that you cleaned; that <u>you were there</u> last night!

Here are a few examples:

- Arranging guest chairs in private offices and table chairs in conference rooms in a pre-set, uniform direction or pattern that it's unmistakably clear someone has done some work here - someone has cleaned!

- Leaving uniform vacuum lines in any area where the type of carpet makes this kind of "look" possible.

- Having the exposed ends of every toilet tissue roll folded to a pro-style "V" like they do in some nice motels/hotels

3. **On the detail cleaning night**, leave one or more professional looking "reminders" customized with your company name to <u>grab</u> the attention of your client in a positive way, and then <u>connect</u> it to YOUR cleaning business <u>reminding</u> them "you've been cleaning" - by gently "poking" them to notice it.

We call them "**<u>NOTICE-able Cleaning Reminders</u>**", and they can be items such as small customized "tent" cards, seat covers, door hangers, easily removable stickers, as well as customized, yet affordable candy dishes and/or flower vases.

Now, let's look at how this NOTICE-able cleaning strategy might look when all the parts are used together:

70. What Does It LOOK Like?

Well, how about …the offices going from "**tired to TERRIFIC**" every Friday (detail visit) by getting completely wiped down stem to stern… not simply dusted, but actually picking up every phone, in-baskets and file, to get it all wiped clean, along with the vents, doors, partition glass and sides of the trash cans.

PLUS… leaving a small professional style, easily removable sticker or note on or near the phone saying basically *"I'm ready to go! I've been completely cleaned and disinfected!"* by your friends at XYZ Cleaning!

Now, how's <u>that</u> for different - NOTICE-able!

Or, how about….the kitchenette going from "**fine to FANTASTIC**" by every Friday going <u>way</u> beyond regular cleaning to NOTICE-able cleaning... by wiping down all cabinet doors, legs of tables and chairs,

PLUS... leaving out a small vase of fresh flowers on the main kitchen counters with a note saying *"Have a great week!"...* from your friends at XYZ Cleaning.

What else?

How about... the carpet going from **"average to AWESOME"** by every Friday vacuuming everything wall-to-wall including under the desks and behind the doors

PLUS... applying a pleasant deodorizer scent to some, or all, of the carpeted offices, lobbies, and conference rooms.

*Or, how about...*the bathroom going from **"so-so to SPARKLING"** by every Friday having all surfaces completely wiped down including partitions, ceiling vents, corners, stainless steel, mirrors, baseboards etc.

PLUS, leaving a small "tent" card saying *"Professionally Cleaned and Sanitized!"...* from your friends at XYZ Cleaning.

Do You Think They Might Notice <u>THAT</u> on Monday?!!!!

We think so too.

By the way.... we all know in many cases, our customers are being bombarded weekly with cleaning companies begging to get a shot at bidding on cleaning their building.

So, here's the 'MILLION DOLLAR' question:

If you can pro-actively create and implement a plan to consistently create a number of moments, even just weekly - where your customer NOTICES your cleaning and is DELIGHTED, what do you think they're likely to do NOW, with those solicitations to bid they get from other cleaning companies during the month?

Yeah, we think so too.

71. Do It PROFITABLY

Fine, you may say,

"But how can I provide this kind of cleaning <u>profitably</u>?"

Fair question. *Let's take a look.*

To begin with, you need to make a <u>shift</u> - a shift in <u>thinking</u> and a shift in <u>hours</u>.

First, the **shift in thinking**:

You need to not only accept that the idea of creating NOTICE-able cleaning makes sense, but that it's worth the initial challenge and awkwardness of putting it into practice.

And that's how we suggest you start - by testing it out at one or two buildings to see <u>how</u> it works and, to prove to yourself that it, in fact, <u>does</u> work!

We'll assume for the sake of time that you're willing to make the shift in thinking.

Next, the **shift in hours**.

You can make a <u>strategic shift of the total hours</u> available for the week. As an example, you might begin to clean most nights with a "basics only", "touch-up" or "light" cleaning approach in mind.

Why?

...to "afford" the hours needed for the labor intensive DETAIL cleaning night!

Let's see what this might look like.

Let's say, a building had been cleaned by one person approx. 3 ½ hrs. per night 5 x/ week, or about 17 ½ hrs./week total.

To achieve a NOTICE-able cleaning schedule with about the same number of hours, you might shift the hours to create the following schedule: 3 hrs. Monday - Thursday of "light" cleaning so you can "afford" to dedicate a full 5 ½ hours for the "DETAIL cleaning" scheduled for Friday.

You'll still coming in at about 17 ½ hrs. per week like the first schedule, but *with a very different approach and effect!*.

NOW, on Monday mornings, you have a <u>great opportunity</u> to delight your customer... when they see the NOTICE-able results of your Friday evening detail cleaning efforts!

It's important, but not easy

Trying to "trim" the cleaning hours from some nights to "find" the needed hours for the DETAIL night... <u>isn't easy</u>.

Trying to "staff" a building with only a few hours most nights and then a lot on one big night set up to deliver NOTICE-able cleaning <u>isn't easy.</u>

Trying to find a way to clean a building on the "basics only" nights without a great number of hours but that gives your customer acceptable cleaning <u>isn't easy either</u>.

But,

<u>What is it worth</u> to finally have the opportunity **to create incredible**

value for your clients by **having a repeatable system in place to consistently create moment after scheduled moment specifically intended to "DELIGHT" your customers**... by having them NOTICE your cleaning?

By the way, there's nothing wrong with wanting your customers to NOTICE your cleaning, the results of you and your staff's many hours of tireless work.

A wise man once said "Everyone has a horn around their neck... and sometimes you have to blow your own horn...or otherwise, it's possible no one else ever will!"

That may sound slightly pushy. But there's a lot of truth in it too.

Your customer <u>wants</u> to be delighted with you and your cleaning company.

Think about that.

Your customer <u>wants</u> to be delighted with you and your cleaning company. But if your <u>current</u> strategy is leaving them flat, bored, "taking you for granted" and not calling other than to complain, then maybe, just maybe...

...you need a NEW strategy!

That's right, you may need to create a NEW cleaning strategy that highlights your work - so not only do you know how much cleaning you and your people have done... but your customer will as well.

And it's all because you had a strategy to make sure they NOTICED.

P.S. And, when you run a cleaning business that consistently delights its clients, you can look at **charging premium prices for your work, and getting more referrals!!!**

72. Be MORE... So They Leave LESS

It simple, but powerful:

Be MORE than just an office cleaning company to your customers. The MORE services you provide for your customer, the LESS likely they are to leave you.

Why?

Well, again, it's human nature.

When your customers rely on you for only one type of cleaning, say, office cleaning, it's not too tough for them to simply replace you with a new contractor.

But, if you take care of multiple responsibilities it becomes <u>much</u> harder for them to replace you. Not impossible...but harder.

Bottom line:

Having not one, but a number of services connecting you to your customers can create a more involved, closer and longer lasting business relationship.

What kind of services are we talking about?

Well, there's a variety of services "cleaning" companies offer. Here are just a few:

- Tile Maintenance

- Exterior Window Cleaning

- Tracking/Ordering/Stocking Consumable Poly/Paper Supplies

- Event/Meeting Set-up and Take Down

- Parking Lot Sweeping

- Grounds Maintenance i.e. removing litter, clearing walks

- Floor Mat/Runner Cleaning

- Carpet Cleaning

- Power Washing

- Watering Plants/ Cleaning Artificial Plants

- Light Repair - Painting

73. When Is A Mistake REALLY Fixed?

It happens; *don't say it doesn't.* It certainly happened to us.

- You break a figurine on someone's desk.

- Your floor crew "forgets" to clean-up everything at the end of a tough strip job, leaving your customer to walk in to find a mess in the morning.

- Your cleaner leaves the <u>back</u> door unlocked to an account one week... only to leave the <u>front</u> door unlocked the <u>very</u> next week.

You do everything you can to avoid making mistakes. You put systems in place to catch 95% of things than can go wrong before they happen... *but still mistakes happen.*

So, how do you know when the mistake is fixed?

(a). Is it fixed when the cleaning person at the job calls to say they fixed it? *No.*

(b). Is it fixed when your Area Supervisor says they checked it out and as far as he can tell, "It's fixed."? *No.*

(c). Is it fixed when you review complaints at the weekly manager's meeting, and pronounce it - "fixed"? *No.*

So, when is it <u>really</u> fixed?

Well, we suggest that it's fixed...<u>when the CUSTOMER says it's fixed</u>... and not a minute before!

Let us give you a quick example.

Let's say one of your people spill something on the carpeting at one of your accounts. And let's also say you're conscientious and promptly take action.

That's right, you call the customer, explain what happened, take full responsibility, apologize for the inconvenience, and clearly explain how you're going to correct it.

Then, you send a floor crew out to spot extract the carpet and they report back to you that it's done.

All set right? *Not necessarily.*

You see, over the years we've had these kinds of mistakes happen and thought we had it "fixed" too, only to have the customer call back the next morning complaining,

"Hey, what's the problem, we thought you guys were going to take care of this carpet spill last night?"

Whoa! We sure didn't expect that!

Well, of course, there may be any number of explanations for what happened.

- Maybe the floor crew did a fast "once over" and the stain "wicked" back up overnight.

- Or maybe they cleaned up the wrong spill; maybe they worked on an entirely <u>different</u> spill, because they didn't read the work sheet correctly.

- Or maybe an employee <u>showed</u> them the "wrong" spill.

- Or maybe the site supervisor <u>forgot</u> to go back and verify that it was cleaned up properly.

It could be any number of things; it really doesn't matter.

What <u>does</u> matter is that the mistake isn't fixed until the customer thinks it's fixed, and so far, this one doesn't!

So, again, we say a mistake is "fixed" when we've done all of our work to correct the situation... <u>and</u> <u>the</u> <u>customer</u> <u>agrees</u> <u>it's</u> <u>fixed</u>.

And to do that second part, you need to....

<u>Follow-up</u> with the customer!

That's right, you need to call back, or stop out, to discuss things, after you've worked on a problem to make sure everyone's looking at the "same thing" - and **to make sure the customer is satisfied the problem is properly and completely fixed!**

Oh, by the way, here's one more "thing" you may want to add to the list of requirements you need to meet before considering a mistake fixed.

Basically, one more "bar" you want to reach.

We used to say that a mistake wasn't "fixed" until our customer not only agreed it was fixed, but that we've were also able to turn around the situation... so we were back in their, for lack of a better term, "good graces" again.

We wanted them to feel as good, or better, about our company <u>after</u>

we fixed the mistake than they did before it happened.

That's an even <u>tougher</u> "bar" to reach, *but it's worth it.*

So, make sure you go the extra mile. That may mean offering a generous credit to their bill or cleaning all their carpet (not just the spot) for FREE.

We say, "It isn't fixed until they're <u>delighted</u> with us, again!" And you won't know <u>that</u> unless you ask.

74. Short, General And Frequent WINS!

That's right, when it comes to **"checking on"** or **inspecting** accounts, *short, general and frequent, beats long, detailed and occasional.*

In the early years, we used to have a formal system of checking our accounts.

It included a rigid schedule, either weekly or monthly, where a manager would be required to fill out a very lengthy and detailed inspection form.

It wasn't a bad system; it just <u>wasn't</u> very <u>good</u>!

You see, long detailed inspections done only occasionally, such as monthly, don't fit very well in our type of work.

Why?

Well, you know as well we do that the janitorial cleaning business can be <u>very</u> fluid. So many things can change from day to day, *including who is actually cleaning the building.*

So, when you only do an inspection monthly, the reality of high employee "turnover" can create problems.

You may literally end up inspecting the cleaning of an employee that's just quit… be reviewing it with his replacement who just started… only to hear him inform you that "Friday's going be his last day!"

Yeah, <u>ouch</u>... talk about ineffective!

And then there's the length and detail of the form you use.

You should keep 'em short and general.

Seriously, who's kidding who? We've seen the longest and most detailed inspection forms, and in our experience, *they're nearly worthless.*

They're overwhelming
<u>nobody</u> wants to complete them,

<u>fewer</u> want to read them... and yeah,

nearly <u>no one</u> acts on them!

Some companies require them; but we've often found it's simply an exercise in *phony*, or at least, <u>misguided "professionalism"</u>; as if simply filling out forms and generating paperwork has value.

It doesn't!

"Lip service" type quality control measures <u>don't</u> have real value - <u>only real quality control does</u>.

And the time and expense of scheduling and performing these overwhelming, *but lame*, documents, is *crazy...* considering they mostly end up in the trash or a file.

You know it and we know it. So, what's the answer?

You need to check your work to consistently deliver reliable and high quality cleaning. Right?

Yes, but do it in a way that's <u>practical</u>, <u>useable</u>, and <u>appropriate</u> for the nature of the work you perform.

75. Treat ALL Customers The Same... *Right?*

The safe answer would be a flat out... Yes!

Well, never ones to play it safe, we'll go ahead and say it**... No!**

Ok, ok, hold your horses...let us explain.

- If you're talking about delivering what you promised, then sure, "Yes".

- Or, if you're talking about showing every customer that you appreciate them...then, "Yes", again.

- And, if you're talking about treating customers fairly... absolutely, "Yes", to that one too!

But......if you're talking about giving every customer:

  -the exact same amount of attention,
  -the exact same number of customer service calls,
  -the exact same number of times when you'll ok extra cleaning,
  for them, at no charge, **then... No !**

You see this "treat every customer the same" idea, only works if all customers are "the same" or close to the same....which, of course, they're not!

Don't believe us?

Years ago, <u>before</u> we started to closely watch the profitability of each account, we had three customers all call in at the same time.

Each one said they needed a bunch of last minute, extra work done right away - that night, because VIP's were coming!

Anyway, we were up to our necks in work already, so this rush of last-minute requests was definitely going to push us "over the edge".

We ended up taking care of two of the customers that night, just like they asked for...but had to tell the third "Sorry, we simply can't get to you tonight."

"You'll have to wait till tomorrow."

As you might expect, that third customer <u>wasn't</u> thrilled.

Here's the thing, a few days later, when we finally got around to looking at the profitability of each of our accounts.

To our surprise....of the two accounts we were able to get to that first night, one was only <u>marginally</u> profitable, and the other one was frankly a financial "<u>money pit</u>" for us!

That's right, we were virtually losing money there every month... and with no real chance of increasing <u>their</u> price or reducing <u>our</u> expenses to turn it around, anytime soon.

But that wasn't the end of the story.

Have you guessed already?

That's right, <u>of course</u>, on the other hand, that <u>third</u> account; you remember the one, where we called to let them know they'd "have to wait"....

Yep, after closer inspection of the numbers, <u>that third one</u> was the <u>only</u> one that was actually profitable. *In fact, quite profitable; a virtual "money machine", churning out profits for us every month!*

195

Ooops!

Boy, we wished we <u>hadn't</u> told <u>them</u> "they'd have to wait!"

Don't get us wrong; we're not suggesting "snubbing your nose" at <u>any</u> customer that's only marginally profitable.

We are saying, however, when laying out the different levels of service you can deliver to different levels of accounts with different levels of profitability, then, as our mothers told us repeatedly...

"For crying out loud, use your head, that's why the good Lord gave it to you!" It's not unethical or poor customer service.

It's survival.

We seem to remember reading an article where a reporter was interviewing the then-popular and well-respected CEO of a large Fortune 100 company.

They asked him "The customer is always right, *right?*"

In so many words, he basically said, "No. You simply cannot give every customer, everything they want, all the time, at whatever price they want...unless you plan on going broke!"

Now, that's not politically correct, is it?

No, we want to *believe*, and more importantly we want to say that we can give <u>all</u> of our customers, <u>everything</u> they want, <u>every</u> time, no matter what!

And we agree, that <u>would</u> be nice; but it isn't *reality*, is it?

At least not all the time.

No, the truth is, you run our cleaning business in the real world with a limited amount of resources; the most important one of which is your people. And the truth is... the best you can do, and what you <u>should</u> challenge yourself to do, is

..to allocate those resources as efficiently as you can to deliver maximum results to your customers **while delivering <u>necessary</u> profitability to your business....**

Yes...necessary!

Yes, you owe your customers what you promised them. No question about it. But you also owe it to yourself, your family and your employees to keep your financial eyes "wide open", so you can **make decisions** that **make money**!

And customers should understand. They run businesses too.

That's right; you're not doing anyone any favors, including your customers, if you're running your cleaning company on financially "thin ice".

76. Have You Got A 3-Hour MAGNET?

Next time you sit down to figure out how many hours to bid a building at, or assign to a cleaner, you may want to remember this story.

Years ago, we picked up a new account; an office building we thought should take about 4 hrs. to clean.

So, when we started the account, we would show someone how to clean it in 4 hrs. And, things went fine the first week.

Our cleaner spent at least the 4 hrs. we gave them, maybe even a little more, since they were new.

Then came the BIG surprise.

As we kept watching the timesheets, we noticed the cleaning times *began to drop.*

Slowly at first; from 4 hrs. to 3 ¾ hrs. within as little as a week, AND then down to maybe 3 ½ after another week or two. And finally, we saw times coming in as low as 3 ¼ . . .or 3 hours!

What in the world was going on?

- Didn't we train them well enough?

- Were they taking shortcuts?

- Was it laziness?

- Did we just overestimate the time needed?

It took a while, but we began to realize something. Drum roll...

Our part time cleaners **liked** to work about 3 hours per night!

Call it 'human nature'.

Call it whatever you want; but we saw it over and over again - our part time cleaning associates' hours would eventually <u>gravitate</u> to about 3 hrs. per night ...*like they were being pulled by a powerful magnet!*

We asked our part-timers about it. They offered all kinds of reasons from:

"After working my day job, we get tired after about 3 hours of cleaning at night." to…

"I don't want to be out too late" and *"I like to be home by 9 P.M."*

In the end, the reasons they gave may not be as important as simply being aware that this 3 hr. *'MAGNET'* exists at all, or at least did in our part-time night operation.

So, what should we do?

We could have fought it, and retrained our folks over and over again until they put in the exact amount of hours we assigned them.

Or, we could try something different - which is what we did.

We decided not to fight this natural tendency, but instead to accept it for what it was, keep an eye on it, and sometimes even find ways to use it to our advantage.

What do we mean?

Well, what would happen if we gave each cleaner as close to 3 hrs. per night, as possible...which is what they seemed to want?

We tried it - we took our total cleaning hours for a building and broke it into as many of these desirable 3 hr. shifts as possible.

For example, a 6 hr. job was now scheduled for two people working 3 hours each.

How did it work?

Fantastic!

Not only did our people like the 3-hour shifts, we quickly discovered those shifts were easier to hire for and keep filled than a shorter (2 hour)... or longer (5 hour) shift.

Bottom line: Check to see if you have an 3-hour MAGNET in your business! If so, make sure it's working for you, not against you.

77. The BEST Time to Raise Your Price

Well, the short answer, of course, may be something like "...when the customer will happily accept it without a fuss".

Sure, sounds simple, but when in the world will that ever happen?

"Not in my lifetime." you might think. Well, maybe...

Maybe not!

Here's an "insider" strategy to successfully raising prices:

It's called TIMING. That's right, timing.

The idea is this. Whenever possible, try to put through a justified price increase when your customer "loves" your current cleaning personnel.

Well, "love" may be too strong a word.

How about... is exceptionally happy with? Or really likes? Or is very satisfied with?

You get the idea; but, why is that so important? What does that have to do with anything?

Well, in our experience...PLENTY.

That's right, in our experience we had found even when we put through a very small yet and very overdue price increase, if our customer was not "altogether" happy with our current cleaner, the new price was about as likely of being accepted, as a snowball's chance in ...you know where.

Why?

Well, because the truth is... PEOPLE make these decisions; not machines; but real "flesh and blood", emotional, sometimes *irrational* people.

And whether you like it or not, or whether you think it's fair or not, when your contact thinks about whether or not to approve your increase, he or she is affected by "things" like **whether or not they and their staff "<u>like</u>" your current cleaner**.

So, how do you know if you have <u>that</u> kind of "highly-appreciated" cleaning associate on your staff?

You know the signs.

They're the ones that get the holiday hams and are invited to the company picnics.

And, when a company has <u>that</u> kind of a loyal relationship with your cleaning person, getting <u>reasonable</u> price increases approved isn't a very tough thing to do.

Heck, we've had buildings where price increases "sailed through" where, the quality of the cleaning our employee was delivering, was, to be fair, good, but not "exceptional".

We had to believe the fact that the customer <u>trusted</u> our cleaner, was <u>comfortable</u> with them being in their building, and may have even considered them to be a <u>friend</u>, played at least some part in explaining why the increase went through so easily.

We understood it wasn't the actual cleaning <u>alone</u> that produced this kind of loyalty.

It was the <u>person</u>.

Let's be clear, we are <u>NOT</u> suggesting taking advantage of any client by putting through an unfairly large increase, nor an increase where one is not justified, *simply because you know they "love" your cleaner.*

Not at all.

But where an increase is called for, knowing if the company has very positive feelings about your cleaning associate and their level of service is something to, at the very least, think about... ahead of time.

We live in the real world. And suggest you do too.

Speaking of which, prepare yourself, because this next tip is about real-world stuff too.

78. How to SURVIVE "Windows Of Vulnerability"

What are these "windows of vulnerability", and why do you need to know how to survive them?

Ok, let's say the cleaning person you have assigned to one of your best accounts for a long time...*has just left to retire.*

Or, let's say, at another one of your buildings, your customer has now assigned the office manager to work with you because the contact "you normally deal with"... *has had his position eliminated.*

Or, let's say, you've promoted the site manager who has been supervising one of your accounts for years ...*to another bigger account.* So, a brand new site manager will be starting.

Or, let's say, your customer calls to let you know some "things" have been coming up missing around the office. They're <u>not</u> saying it's your people...*but they just wanted to let you know.*

Or, let's say, while trying to get your customer ready for some VIP's coming in for a meeting, your floor crew accidentally knocked an ornamental keepsake off ... *one of the big bosses' desks.*

Ok, that's enough examples.

<u>These</u> are the kinds of "windows of vulnerability" we're talking about.

And, you can make the case in nearly every one of the examples above, that it's no one's <u>fault</u>.

For example, when your cleaning associate assigned to a building has to <u>be moved</u>, <u>gets promoted</u> or <u>decides to retire</u>, you could say that isn't anyone's *fault*....so nothing to worry about...right?

Not so fast.

You might like to think of it *that way*, and just get back to business as usual.

Better think again, because.... **"fault" is <u>not</u> all that matters here, or, at least, may not be the most important thing!**

And when a "window of vulnerability" appears in your cleaning business, it's best to treat things as anything <u>but</u> business-as-usual!

Again, fault isn't the issue.

In some important ways, it doesn't matter if the reason for it happening had <u>anything</u> to do with you at all.

The fact is, it <u>did</u> happen, and you're going to have to deal with it, by considering...

...what your customer may be **thinking and feeling.**

And what is that? Well, let's take a quick look, shall we....

The cleaning lady they've <u>known and trusted</u> for years is leaving to retire - that's CHANGE.

And that change may make them feel very <u>nervous</u> about who you're planning to replace that person with. Or, they may start to feel you can't control turnover.

The new person, of course, will be a "stranger' to them at first, as any new person would be. And it doesn't matter if it makes any sense or not, the fact is, it's CHANGE... and it can make them uncomfortable!

Here's a hint; you don't want your customers feeling uneasy or uncomfortable, at least not about you, and not for very long!

It's not necessarily *logical*. It doesn't matter.

It's change; and sometimes, many times, any change at all, can send up "red flags" for your customers, along with their radar to watch the cleaning!

Real quickly, let's look at an example...

Let's say, you're told you have a new contact to report to at a building you clean.

And, let's say, you've just promoted a site supervisor (Rose) moving her from that account to a different site, AND suddenly you begin to hear your new contact say to you little things like...

"Boy, I don't know, we sure hated to lose Rose; people say things just don't seem the same around here since you guys moved her."

You may start to hear these kinds of comments after only a couple of days - after you make a personnel "move"...as your customer begins to **miss** the way it was... and **complain** about how it is now.

What can you do to survive these "windows of vulnerability? Here are a few tips:

- First, always keep in touch with your customers, but stay in **even closer** contact when you face a "window of vulnerability".

- Second, listen to your customer. Be sure to listen for what they're **feeling**... especially when these changes happen.

- Third, <u>reassure</u> you customer not only that you understand their concerns, but that you have a **plan** to make sure things work out smoothly for them.

- Fourth, continue to <u>stay "on top"</u> of the situation and in touch with your customer, until you, and your customer, are **convinced** things are "well in hand" again.

79. I Can't Believe We LOST The Account!

It happens.

We don't want it to, but it happens - we lose an account.

And when it happens, after getting "the call" or the letter informing you that you're being replaced, have you ever had the words, "I can't believe we lost the account!" <u>pounding</u> in your head?

We have.

And if you've been in the cleaning business for any length of time, you have too. If you haven't, we're happy for you, but don't kid yourself, you will.

Sometimes losing an account (job) <u>doesn't</u> have to do with things "within your control".

There, you'll just have to move on.

Other times, it does have to do with things that <u>were</u> "within your control"...... and that's when you <u>should</u> feel bad.

Think about it, if you're a professional, who takes pride in the service you deliver to your clients, then, of course you would feel bad.

It's the natural response when you or one of your people "drops the ball" and you end up losing a valued client.

It's supposed to hurt.

In fact, at least for us, and many other cleaning contractors we've spoken with over the years, it hurts the same, no matter how long you've been in business.

It hurts as much if the customer is big or little. And it hurts no matter how long you've had them.

It just hurts.

And at <u>those</u> times, when it <u>is</u> your fault, and you get "the call" letting you know you're out, you need to do a "gut" check <u>and</u> a "systems" check to see where things broke down.

This is your job, to take "the hit", try to salvage the client if you can, but either way, diagnose the problem to find out where your systems failed.

- Was it your QC systems, or lack thereof?

- Was it your Customer Service systems, or lack thereof?

- Was it your HR systems, or lack thereof?

You get the idea, and you can determine pretty quickly what needs to be done.

That' right, it's time for the "heavy lifting" of figuring out what went wrong and what it's going to take, to keep it from happening in the future. (That's why you get paid the "big bucks", you're the boss; and <u>this</u> is when you earn your money.)

However, the very fact that you're going to lose accounts, whether or not it's your fault, should be reason enough to commit yourself to

<u>always</u> having an active, ongoing marketing campaign.

By the way, a couple more "things"...

We remember seeing a cleaning company that proudly advertised "And we still have our <u>first</u> customer!" implying they're so good... *they never lose a customer!*

Of course, we always wanted to ask, if they still had their 3rd, 14th, and 38th customers... *but we guess that could have burst their marketing and advertising bubble!*

Frankly, it's a 'bunch of malarkey'.

It's the same cleaning guys who so proudly fly the whole "We <u>never</u> miss a trash!" marketing banner.

We say, "It falls on deaf ears!"

Your prospects aren't stupid. And while we're on the topic don't <u>even</u> get us started on the whole ...

"Take the <u>white glove</u> we've enclosed in the envelope, wipe it all over your building, and if you get any dirt on it, call us because we wouldn't <u>ever</u> let that happen!" gimmick.

Yeah, we think *"Elvis left the building"* a long time ago on <u>that</u> sorry excuse for a marketing message too!

INSIDER SECRET #7
Create Systems To Go "Auto Pilot"

80. RULES? You're Gonna Need 'Em!

We were going to be different.

That's right. When we first started, we decided we were going to be the cleaning company with a "heart".

We were determined to treat our cleaning associates with <u>more</u> than respect, we wanted to go the "extra mile", and treat everyone like "family".

Well, in time, we discovered sometimes a company, like a "healthy" family has to practice some "tough love" by having, dare we say it - **rules!**

Here's how it went...

In the early years, when we were first starting out, we'd give out employee pay advances pretty freely.

For example, if one of our cleaners was in a financial "pickle", let's say, needed help to make a down payment on a car, or rent an apartment, we would generally be willing to give them a pay advance of $100 or more, to help them make it through the "occasional" tough patch.

And things went ok... for a while.

But, as time went on, and we began to grow, we soon found ourselves with a longer and longer list of associates with larger and larger outstanding pay advances.

And the list of reasons given as *"emergencies"* grew too.

In fact, not long after that, we began to realize as soon as someone paid off their "first" advance, they would somehow "magically" need to have another one take its place... only this time more than the first one, and, of course, right away!

That's right, the balance on these pay advances grew rapidly as our associates started to "add on" to their current advance with another advance!

Can you see where this is going?

It became unmanageable.

That's right! We soon began to feel like the local bank, credit card company, or pay-day loan office, *except we weren't charging any fees or interest!*

It quickly became obvious that our "good intentions", without the necessary limits and rules, had things spinning out of control; leaving us with a mess on our hands.

Long story short - while honoring our existing pay advances to employees, we put a stop to any new ones.

It took a month or two for our folks to get used to the new "no pay advance" policy, but everyone eventually did; and we got back to being a cleaning company.

Any lessons here?

Well, sure. We learned, for example, that sometimes those "big companies" whose rules we had so often ridiculed, may actually have had some pretty darn good reasons for having them!

And just as importantly, **we learned it <u>doesn't</u> make you insensitive or uncaring to have rules.**

In fact, for those of you who are parents, it's a lot like raising a family; *you won't get kids to say it*, but they <u>need</u> rules, and deep down most would admit they actually <u>want</u> them.

Look at places where rules could help your cleaning business, such as in HR matters like attendance and tardiness etc. Be sure those rules are fair and consistent; and don't be afraid to ask an HR expert or attorney if you need an opinion.

And here's some good news...

<u>Having workplace rules makes it easier to manage your operation today, and avoid some of the "growing pains" of running a bigger company tomorrow.</u>

81. Systems? Yeah, You're Gonna Need Those Too!

In addition to rules, you're going to need systems.

What kind of systems? How to create them? And what they can do for you!

Well, here's how it happened for us...

When we were first starting off, if we were getting ready to go to a brand new account, we would simply grab all the people, supplies and equipment we *thought* we'd need... jump in the van... and go!

Sounds simple - and, it was. It just wasn't effective.

You see we'd have <u>problems</u>:

1. Some cleaning people we took to the account would end up simply wandering around doing little to nothing. Why?

   Well, any number of reasons.

   Either they weren't trained properly in the first place, didn't know how to handle the first day at a new account, or simply weren't being given enough direction by our supervisor.

2. We would always find ourselves missing some important piece of equipment or cleaning supply... so we'd end up having to send somebody back to the shop to get it.

   The reason for this, of course, is we didn't have any pre-set list of supplies and equipment to be sure to bring with us.

3. And finally, we would always seem to forget to lock a door, get a trash or turn off a set of lights.... We simply didn't have a set of rules and procedures that needed to be followed.

We didn't have a SYSTEM.

So, we worked on it. And ultimately, we created a series of systems such as:

- Developing a multiple-step training program for every cleaning associate to go through.

- Creating a checklist for supplies and equipment necessary to bring to a new account.

- Maintaining a log of the important operational information we learned about each account.

- Designing a detailed plan to follow for the start up of any new account.

So, that's what systems can very often look like - *a pre-set number of procedures and practices to follow for any number of situations.*

And you know, as well as we do, there are lots of *situations* to deal with in cleaning. But SYSTEMS can go a long way in efficiently managing these situations.

- Whether it's a system to handle a customer complaint or a client testimonial.

- Whether it's a system to handle a start up of a new account or start up of a new employee

- Whether it's a system for checking the quality of a building or for checking the appearance of your own office.

- Whether it's for the maintenance of your company vehicles or the maintenance of your company records and files.

What kind of systems should they be?

Well, ones that are well thought out, address the situation the <u>way</u> you want, get the desired <u>results</u> you want... and can be understood by anyone and everyone... every time!

Will there be exceptions?

Sure, you'll never be able to completely eliminate times when a situation calls for you to be flexible and vary from your system.

But, if you can stick to your 'well planned out' system 95% of the time, you, my friend, are ahead of the game.

Way ahead. ...Don't believe us?

Just look at the number of so called service companies, including cleaning companies that never seem to get it right. You've seen them:

- They're the ones always forgetting to bring something.

- They're the ones always missing a trash, light or lock.

- They're the ones always neglecting to make a call.

- They're ones always losing the paperwork?

The problem isn't that these problems occur. It's that no one takes the time to resolve them in a way that <u>keeps them solved</u>.

82. Run It... Like You're SELLING It

Have you ever noticed someone in your neighborhood getting ready to put their house up for sale?

You know the drill...

They start banging off a list of things to fix, patch, putty or paint "like crazy". In fact, you can't <u>ever</u> remember seeing them work this hard in any of the time they lived there.

You'll see them replacing badly worn carpeting, trimming bushes, fixing leaky sinks, repairing loose stair steps, as well as painting walls and doors.

Anything and everything to get their house in "ready to show" condition, so prospective buyers see it in the best "light" possible.

In fact, the old joke among these motivated sellers, as they go about rejuvenating their homes for sale is, *"Heck, if we knew it could look this good, we would've stayed!"*

Funny, sure, but there's a lot of truth in it too.

Getting your house ready for sale, and then keeping it looking that way… gives you your best chance at getting "top dollar".

Well, as you might have guessed, we suggest you take the same approach to running your business.

Run your cleaning business like you're getting ready to sell it… and you stand the best chance of not only getting "top dollar" when you do sell it, but of getting the most out of it NOW while you still own it!

What do we mean?

Well, if whenever you make decisions about your cleaning company, you always keep in mind what a prospective buyer would be looking for in a professional, profitable and efficient business to buy, you'll find yourself making better decisions.

And what are those?

Ones that create VALUE

You may decide to put in place any number of systems, practices, and checklists, etc. designed to, as we often say, **"force order onto chaos."**

- For example, in expense control, you may want to start using an automated timekeeping system.

- In <u>marketing</u>, you may want to prepare a series of marketing messages to be delivered on a pre-set schedule and to be delivered in a variety of forms.

You can, and should, look at <u>each</u> <u>part</u> of your company... and see what you can do to shape it more like what it is... a business.

What parts?

Well, let's see - marketing, for sure; but also, hiring, selection, training, inspecting, accounting reporting, motivation, rewarding, equipment, customer service... the list goes on and on.

If you do this "heavy lifting" now, you'll find you have a company that will not only bring "top dollar" down the road, but will operate profitably until that day comes.

And, it will be one that your employees will be <u>proud</u> to work in.

Enjoy a well run company now. Don't wait to fix it up until the very end when you're trying to sell, and catch yourself saying ...

"Heck, if I knew my cleaning business could run this smoothly, I would've kept it!"

83. Lawyer Is NOT A Dirty Word

Ever heard the expression, "If you want to be successful, watch what everyone else is doing... and do the <u>opposite</u>"?

We don't think that's always true, but it certainly is true a lot of the time... and here's an important example - lawyers.

That's right. LAWYERS.

To listen to the average person talk about lawyers you'd think they were single-handedly the cause of the fall of western civilization.

Be honest. Haven't you heard that? In fact, can you even think of a time or two, when you may have said something like that yourself?

Probably; we all have. Why?

Well, think about this. What words do you hear people use to describe lawyers?

Scoundrels, vultures... and worse, right?!

Well, it would be easy to jump on the band wagon... and simply join in and agree that... 'they're a bunch of crooks'.

But we can't. And we can't because we know better.

Don't get us wrong.

Some of them certainly act like a bunch of overpaid *vultures*. <u>Maybe</u> even a larger percentage than in other professions.

But not <u>all</u> of them... not by a long shot

And frankly, contrary to popular opinion, many of them are honest, smart and hardworking. On top of that, they may be one of the *best kept secrets* to keeping your cleaning company on the fast track.

Shocking? Don't believe it? Ok, but let us tell you a quick story.

For years, every now and then, we would come across a "touchy" HR (personnel) situation.

Now, don't get us wrong, we already had an HR manager, and a number of policies and practices in place. But, sometimes, things just don't fit neatly into the rules.

For example, sometimes we would get stuck, not knowing whether or not we could legally terminate an employee we had been having trouble with.

We had lots of questions swirling in our heads, but with <u>no</u> confidence we had any good answers for them... we were virtually <u>immobilized</u> - stuck, not knowing what to do!

Questions like....

- Did we have all of our legal "ducks in a row"?

- Were we on a firm legal footing if we let the person go?

- How should we handle the corrective interview?

And for a long time, we would simply do nothing when we were faced with these "sticky" situations. We would stumble around at work like *zombies,* upset about the situation, but without a clue of what to do about it.

Ever been there?

Anyway, long story short, we got in touch with an attorney who specialized in employment law. This lawyer became a great legal advisor to us.

Anytime we were stuck, our lawyer, yes lawyer, quickly got us un-stuck by giving us the to-the-point legal advice we needed - to get over it or through it - and back on track.

We know. We know. But isn't it expensive getting advice from an attorney?

Yes, it can be.

But, it can be <u>more</u> expensive if you can't get past those inevitable personnel problems everyone is bound to face at one time or another.

The sales we landed and the money we made by getting <u>unstuck</u> far outweighed the few hundred dollars we had to pay for good legal advice now and then.

By the way, this same idea also holds true for other kinds of advice as well, such as accounting. (Can you say CPA?).

Ok, that's it. We won't say anything else nice about lawyers. We wouldn't want it to "go to their heads".

84. Does YOUR Office Need A New Cleaning Company?

We hope not.

We hope <u>your</u> office or building is a shining example of the very best your company can deliver.

But if it isn't... it should be.

Really, it's just "not ok" to deliver quality cleaning to your clients, and then have your office look like a "frat house" on a Sunday morning.... *after a Saturday night!*

We read somewhere General Schwarzkopf had said that polished shoes were critical to success in his mind.

The idea being that if you start allowing yourself to deliver less than the best, it's more likely you'll struggle, *at other times*... as in war or times of crisis...when you can't afford to not be at your best!

That's right, when it comes to the appearance of our office we follow the old expression..."Look Sharp - Be Sharp!"

And, we went as far as to <u>advertising</u> the point!

Really! We created a marketing piece which we sent to our target market with a photo of our office building and a huge headline *challenging* readers with the following question:

"Would <u>your</u> current cleaning company be <u>comfortable</u> if you stopped by, *unannounced*, to see the cleanliness of <u>their</u> office?"

Yeah, <u>that</u> got their attention!

And in the marketing piece, we went on, of course, to invite them to stop by to see our building… <u>anytime</u>!

We made what other companies saw as a "pain in the neck"… namely, taking care of their own facility, **into *a competitive advantage!***

You can too!

One final thought, forgetting completely about the amount of positive marketing "mileage" you can generate with this strategy... think about this:

What effect do you think having your office looking "sharp as a tack" has on applicants that "come in" to your office, and on employees that "head out" of your office for a night of cleaning?

You know the answer.

So, don't miss out on all the benefits of having a spotlessly clean and well maintained office, especially when**... you <u>already</u> know a cleaning company that can handle the job!!**

85. STOP Wasting Your Time

Today can be unforgiving.

There isn't a lot of time to waste; not anymore.

We ran into a friend who runs a car dealership one day. His dad use to run a dealership, before retiring a few years ago.

We asked him how things were now, compared to when his dad was in the business. And he explained that today, there's no time to be *strolling around the dealership smoking a cigar*, like his dad used to do in the old days.

He went on to make the point that today you'd better be "on the ball" all the time, or you risk getting run over by your competition!

Sound familiar?

Well, here's one practical way to save valuable time starting today.

Years ago, when we would get a call from a business asking for a quote on their cleaning, we would simply jot down their name, confirm their address, and set up a time and date for a walk through.

Good so far, right?

We thought so too, until one day when we had an appointment to bid a building out of town, and upon arriving, we began to ask a few questions such as:

- How many times per week would you like to be cleaned?

- When can we come in to do the cleaning?

- What kinds of cleaning services do you need included?

You see, we were targeting accounts where we could provide 3-5 times per week office cleaning in the early evening from, let's say, 6:00 - 9:30 PM.

So, we were more than a little shocked when we heard the prospect answer our questions by saying…

"Oh no, we <u>don't</u> need any <u>regular</u> office cleaning. We're just taking quotes on getting our lunchroom floor stripped!"

We thought to ourselves…

What, you've got to be kidding!

This isn't the kind of work we were looking for; but, we only had ourselves to blame.

You see, we <u>assumed</u> because they were on our targeted list of companies that <u>naturally</u> they would still be good prospects for our regular office cleaning.

Our <u>mistake</u> was, of course, we forgot to qualify the lead, by asking a few questions on the phone when they first called in, to verify they were actually a good prospective client for us.

Unfortunately, we "jumped the gun" like this several times before eventually having to face the error of our ways - **by finding ourselves** ***over an hour from our office, at an account we had no business bidding on!***

And all because we didn't take one minute to make sure we were on the "same page".

We can tell you it was a long ride back heading back to our office on those icy roads!

But that was the last time.

86. The Power of IMPLEMENTATION

Take your pick:

1. The question isn't "what <u>can</u> you do?"… the question is "what <u>will</u> you do?"

2. "Quit <u>talking</u>, and start <u>doing</u>!"

3. And, of course, our *personal* favorite, "<u>Talk</u> is cheap...*whiskey costs money!*"

What is the message of all three? Stated simply:

The difference between dreams and achievement is IMPLEMENTATION.

And how quickly and efficiently we implement our ideas determines, to a great degree, how fast we will improve, and how soon we'll begin to see results.

Implement important ideas quickly… and in a short time you're likely to see results.

Plod along, and take what seems like "forever to implement ideas" and... well, you aren't likely to see much improvement in what also might begin to seem like...*forever!*

And this drive to IMPLEMENT can change your day from the slow drudgery of work… into an exciting challenge.

It's not fun to be "just getting by".

It's not fun to be struggling today; facing the likelihood that tomorrow won't be much better.

Fortunately, that doesn't have to be you, because you can change your future - by changing what you do with your present.

Starting today.... you can commit yourself to taking one good idea at a time, and seeing to it that you get it implemented.

It may be something as simple as "training someone, other than you, to handle customer service calls that come in during the day."

Get that one idea implemented, and you'll have freed up time - time you can use to work on implementing more ideas, faster.

That's right, you can enjoy a "snowball effect" to this "implementation thing" - start getting things in place and you'll find you're getting more done and quicker than ever before.

Don't be one of the folks that when asked how their day was, weakly sighs "Oh, ok, I guess, we got through it."

No, you can be the exception.

You can be the one to "shake things up"- by actually implementing your ideas.

Don't worry about messing things up when you start implementing your ideas -You will! It's normal.

And that's not what matters in the end anyway!

YOU CAN ALWAYS FIX MISTAKES. They're simply an occupational inconvenience to people who "make things happen"!

87. FINALLY, Meetings That Aren't A Waste

First of all, there's a time for "shooting the bull".

We mean, if you don't take some time each day to "touch base" with your people, just to "visit", a*t least for a little while*, well you're really "missing the boat" and half the fun of owning a cleaning company.

That's right, if you're not already, you should start making room for some laughs at work....even in meetings.

Honestly, some of the best times we can remember, happened in our weekly staff meetings.

One person after another would start telling their own "You won't believe what happened last night" stories about an employee or customer situation. And, before you know it...

We're all "in tears", crying with laughter.

Now, we'll be the first to admit, a lot of the time, it was *nervous laughter*, but it was definitely a welcome relief.

Yep... good times. But, here's the thing.

We <u>also</u> get a lot of done at those meetings.

- Problems were identified.

- Solutions were suggested.

- Decisions were made.

- Plans were prepared.

- Responsibilities were assigned.

- Progress was checked.

You see, in order to get results from meetings, you need to change what you **expect** from yourself and your staff…<u>at the meeting</u>.

First, of course, you need to be **<u>prepared</u>** for the meeting.

What areas do you want to cover, and in what order?

- Human Resources/ Staffing

- Sales & Marketing

- Operations Accounting

- Customer Service

- Quality Control

- Safety & Security

- Equipment, Chemicals,

- Vehicles Maintenance etc.

And as you might've guessed…you should have a strategic plan for improving <u>each</u> of them.

Here's the tip:

You want to **<u>assign</u>** someone, or some group, to be responsible for making that progress happen.

You need "a way" of **<u>checking and tracking</u>** the progress for each of the plans you've laid out.

And finally, of course, for that, you need to have a way of **<u>measuring</u>** that progress. That's how you'll be able to:

1. *Encourage* and *re-direct*… when progress isn't being made.

2. *Recognize* and *reward*… when progress is being made.

88. Want It Done Right? DON'T Do It Yourself!

No, you didn't misread.

If you want it done right, you shouldn't do it yourself, *or at least not for long!*

We realize that goes against nearly everything you've been told your whole life. But here's the thing...the whole idea that you, and only you, can be counted on to get it right.....*is wrong!*

Try to avoid being limited or short sighted in your view - thinking that you and only you, can be counted on to come through when the "chips are down" or "when it really counts".

Let's be frank.

Here's the way we used to try to think about it when we owned our cleaning business:

If, *God forbid*, either one, or both of us were hit by a bus, and wouldn't be around to:

- help make one decision

- clean one account

- inspect one building

- call one customer

- or send out even one invoice....

To be responsible to our employees and our families, the business had to continue to run the same as ever!

It's sounds harsh, but it's really not.

Honestly, we were proud to be able to say everything would continue to operate just as smoothly even though we weren't there to make sure it all happened.

Now, obviously, even though we were set up to handle that possibility, didn't mean we sat around at work with nothing to do.

No, instead, we tried as much as possible to spend our time working, as they say "on our business, not in it" because we knew that's how we would reach our next goal and our next goal, and so on.

And, by the way, we knew many of our people were better, sometimes much better, than the two of us, at many parts of the business. For example,

- Many or our associates could clean circles around us.

- Our Customer Service Manager had more patience when listening to customer problems than both of us combined.

- Our HR Manager had more experience and tact when handling employee problems than either one of us.

- Our floor maintenance techs could strip and refinish a floor a lot better than either of us could.

We weren't embarrassed of ourselves…**we were proud of them!**

You don't need to be the best technical person in every part of a cleaning operation to run a great cleaning company.

You do, however, need to be the best owner-operator of a cleaning business you can possibly be.

And that calls for different skills like goal setting, motivating employees, as well as creating systems to monitor and measure results.

When you can count on your people to deliver when you need something "done right"… you'll know you're doing something right!

Final Thought

89. What One Man Can Do, Another Can Do

In the movie, *The Edge*, the character played by actor Anthony Hopkins, finds himself stranded in the wilderness. He desperately struggles to survive; having to face one life-threatening situation after another.

His <u>only</u> chance of making it out alive is to implement survival strategies he has, to this point…. **only read about in books**.

But, he <u>does</u> implement them - and <u>it saves his life.</u>

Here are the powerful words he says to himself *over and over* again during the ordeal to stay motivated and focused…..

"What <u>one</u> man can do, <u>another</u> can do!"

"What <u>one</u> man can do, <u>another</u> can do!"

We have done this! <u>YOU can do this!</u> You <u>can</u> create the kind of cleaning business you've always dreamed of. At Clean Guru, we're here, ready to help you "Discover the Guru… in You!"

Our Story:

"Embarrassing, shocking or just plain FUNNY ... you be the judge."

Tony and I were high school friends.

Our dad's were both barbers, who worked together. That's right, honest to goodness, old-fashioned, "pole out in front of the shop" barbers, for the auto factory workers in Toledo, Ohio, just an hour south of Detroit.

Yes, you heard right, <u>that</u> Toledo; hometown of the world famous 'Jeep', and for those of who you remember, Jamie Farr, the *dress-wearing*, wacky *Corporal Klinger*, from the hit TV show M.A.S.H.

Anyway, after working in regular jobs for years, and seeing first hand the frightening lack of job security in the auto industry, Tony and I were determined not to spend the next 30 years working for someone else.

We dreamed of running our own business someday but didn't have the "deep pockets" needed to make our dreams come true!

So, we looked for a business that didn't take much money to get started in. We looked at all kinds of businesses, but every one of them wanted a whole lot more than the two of us had.

Then one day...**we got lucky!**

It turns out a very small cleaning company was up for sale by a guy, who it just so happened, wanted to get out of the cleaning business (... it wouldn't take us long to figure out why!)

We sold everything we could think of to come up with the down payment. The rest, we'd pay to the owner in monthly installments.

We Thought We'd Died... And Gone To Heaven!

Unfortunately, we quickly realized - <u>we only had the first part right</u>. That's right, here's the **bad news**...

We spent all of our money to come up with the down payment. So when the very first payroll came due along with the rest of the bills, we had to use **credit cards** just to get by.

That was scary enough, but there was more....

First, of course, was our new name. Yep, **Dan** and **Tony's** new company was called ... <u>**Jim's**</u> **Cleaning**!

Not very convenient, was it?

That's right! There we were - two guys, running a small, chaotic cleaning company with no money, no experience and really "no business being in business!"

Anything else? .. you might ask. Oh yeah, there's more...

Did I mention that Tony **hates people**?

Well, that's not <u>exactly</u> right, it's people problems he can't stand. And he sure wasn't excited about having a bunch of employees to deal with.

See, Tony's a "computer geek". He likes numbers and systems and order - stuff like that. I know, I know, why in the world would a guy like that even think about, let alone get into, a people business like cleaning. Well, let's just say...

He's a good friend... and I talked him into it!

As for me, as much as Tony hates people problems, I hate computers. I thought they'd go away…they didn't.

Anyway, back to the story…

Well, we regularly worked till late at night, and then had to get in first thing in the morning just to fix any problems from the night before.

And there were always problems.

What else? Well, there was <u>never</u> enough money. At one point …

We were over **$20,000.00** in debt on credit cards!!

And, that doesn't even count how much we owed Jim, the prior owner of the business. That's right, the truth is we had a huge loan with him too. Ugh!

And, of course, he still expected his payment every month… no exceptions! It nearly killed us every month trying to make that payment, but we knew we had to, or we'd be in default and could lose everything.

But there was <u>still</u> more…

How were we doing getting good help? We'll, let's just say we'd place ads, and many times, **no one even showed up** to interview!

What about the employees we <u>did</u> have?

Well, even though we were short handed, we'd still have to deal with some really "bad eggs". I remember one night in particular in the early days.

I'll never forget walking up to confront an employee about why he was a "no call-no show" the night before, only to hear his answer…."Oh yeah, man, sorry, I was **too stoned to work!**"

Oh, great, <u>there's</u> a reassuring answer!

What in the world had we got ourselves into?

And <u>just</u> when you thought it couldn't get any worse… you guessed it … it did!

First, our "dependable fleet" made up of a **"couple old cars and a horse trailer"**, which we used to transport scrubbers and wet vacs, was slowly but surely falling apart!

Then our "loyal" receptionist stole thousands of dollars right out from underneath our noses! (The only bright side being…we **finally** figured out why we couldn't find the postage stamps & office supplies the <u>handwritten</u> "receipts" said we had!)

But at least we had our accounts. I mean, at least we had our *loyal* customers, **right?**

Well, back in those early days, we counted on a couple big industrial accounts just to stay afloat, so we **nervously "babied"** them night and day, so they'd stay with us.

And they were loyal… right up to the day they **dropped us like a rock**…with NO NOTICE; the reason being something like "Well, the owner's kids want to try to do the cleaning for a while because… as they would so kindly put it…

"I mean, how tough could it be, right?"

We were completely burned out, financially wiped out and basically, holding on by a thread. And we'd have gotten out completely, if we could have. But to sell a business - someone has to want to buy it… but, of course, no one did.

I think I can hear you saying, **"STOP! Enough already!"**

Ok, you're right.

The good news is…. that was not the end of our story!!

Suddenly everything changed!

We discovered powerful NEW strategies! We learned amazing "things" we'd never known before. And we turned those "things" into automatic systems that changed our lives completely.

So, What HAPPENED?

✓ Well, Tony and I stayed friends.

✓ We built a cleaning company that delivered over $2,000,000/yr. in office cleaning and related services!

✓ We had a steady stream of profitable business coming in every year.

✓ We had systems to run virtually every part of the business so it could run profitably and smoothly every day… without us!

IMPORTANT UPDATE:

In 2008, we sold our cleaning company - which provided us with lasting financial security. That allows us to work full time helping other cleaning businesses compete and win against the "big" guys!

But, I don't tell you this to brag. Not at all, **I tell you this to show you the truth.**

The Truth Is If We Can Do It …You Can Do It Too!

It's still all out there for you, just like it was for us. We learned a lot in our over 20 years in the cleaning business.

Now, we feel we have a mission.

We were in your shoes not so long ago. Now, we have set off on a mission to help others, who may be struggling like we did. We want to give **YOU everything we know about how to grow, get profitable... and stay profitable!**

We know it's tough out there. And it's getting tougher. But, you can still WIN like we did. And we want to show you how.

Let's start by "leveling the playing field"

That's right, we want as many start-up, small and mid-size cleaning contractors as possible to **compete and win** against the price-cutting "big guys".

Now, here's the powerful 1st step - the CleanBid® Program!

We struggled for years trying to find an effective, affordable and easy-to-understand method to create janitorial cleaning bids. We looked to other cleaning companies and industry experts for help, but were disappointed with what we found.

We were determined to find a solution for cleaning companies with a simple, affordable, and competitive way to create professional estimates and bids.

NOW, it's a reality with the....CleanBid® Program.

That's right! Check out the demo and see for yourself if it isn't the easiest, yet most amazing bidding system you've ever seen. And the best thing is it's online and ready for you 24/7, anytime you want to bid a janitorial cleaning job.

It comes pre-loaded...

with industry specific cleaning tasks and gives you everything you need including **price recommendations** and amazing **ready-to-deliver proposals & reports.**

Soon, we'll be offering even more products and services that specifically target the biggest problems in growing your company:- *HOW TO GET AND KEEP MORE PROFITABLE ACCOUNTS*.

Enough talk. Today is your day!

Make it a day you decided to make a change for the better. Check out the FREE demo to see just how quickly and easily you'll be able to bid cleaning jobs from now on using the CleanBid® Program.

Visit us NOW at www.CleanBid.net

CPSIA information can be obtained
at www.ICGtesting.com
Printed in the USA
BVOW06*0126191017
498129BV00007B/23/P